Surviving Local Property Tax

Surviving Local Property Tax

Brian Keegan, Mary Roche and
Norah Collender

Chartered
Accountants
Ireland

Published in 2014 by
Chartered Accountants Ireland
Chartered Accountants House
47–49 Pearse Street
Dublin 2
www.charteredaccountants.ie

ISBN 978-1-908199-73-7

Typeset by Datapage
Printed by Turner's Printing Company, Longford, Ireland

Contents

1

Introduction

Successive governments over the last 30 years have found it difficult to introduce a property tax. A residential property tax introduced in the 1980s was abolished within 20 years. An even shorter-lived farm tax was abolished before it achieved any significant yield. Even the immediate predecessor to Local Property Tax (LPT), known as the Household Charge, was not fully complied with.

It seems, however, that in its first year this Local Property Tax has achieved widespread compliance and yields exceeding the amounts which had been forecast. While the concept behind LPT is simple – one person accounting for one tax per property based on the value – it is underpinned by a comprehensive and complex piece of legislation. The purpose of this book is to explain how the legislation works, to point out the pitfalls and to try and bring some clarity to the sometimes convoluted wordings needed in law to enforce the tax.

Rather than rely solely on narrative explanation, we have used many examples to illustrate how aspects of the legislation work. We have also included a detailed section-by-section analysis of the Local Property Tax legislation (the Finance (Local Property Tax) Act 2012 (as amended by the Finance (Local Property Tax) (Amendment) Act 2013) (the 'Act') to show you how the whole system interrelates. The success of the LPT in 2013 suggests that this tax will be with us for many years to come. Local Property Tax is administered by the Office of the Revenue Commissioners, so many of their powers and procedures have become part of its legal framework.

As property changes hands, and as time moves on, new scenarios will arise. We hope you will find this book useful as you deal with these scenarios.

2

Liability for Local Property Tax

2.1 Who is Liable for Local Property Tax?

The "liable person" in respect of a "residential property" at the "liability date" is required to pay LPT, based on the "chargeable value" of the residential property as of the "valuation date".

So, who is a liable person? Under tax law a "person" is not just a natural person or an individual, but also includes a company, a partnership or a trust. It is likely that the liable person, in most cases, will be the owner of the property but the definition of liable person is quite broad (*section 11*). Having a beneficial interest in a residential property by way of occupancy or tenancy can make a person liable to local property tax even if there is no ownership. A **liable person** as defined includes the following:

- the owner/s of residential property in Ireland (irrespective of whether they are resident in Ireland or not);

- holders of an exclusive right of residence (not shared) in a residential property, e.g. a life interest;

EXAMPLE

Una Malone lives alone in a house that is owned by her daughter Lucy. While Lucy is the legal registered owner of the property, under the terms of her late husband's will Una has a right of residence in the property and is therefore liable for LPT.

However, if Una lives in the house with her daughter Lucy, then Lucy is solely liable for LPT as Una's interest in the property is not counted for the purposes of LPT because Una does not have an **exclusive** right of residence.

- persons with a long-term right of residence (for life or for 20 years or more) which entitles them to exclude any other person from the property;

- lessees who hold long-term leases of residential property (for 20 years or more);

EXAMPLE

Joe Jackson owns a residential property, which is leased on the 1 May 2013 under a two-year lease. Joe is the liable person for LPT due for 2013 and for 2014 (liability date 1 November 2013). On 1 October 2014, he enters into a lease of 25 years with a tenant called Emily Moore. As Emily is a lessee with a long-term leasehold interest in the property on 1 November 2014 (the liability date for 2015), she is the liable person for LPT for 2015 and thereafter.

- landlords where the property is rented under a short-term lease (for less than 20 years);

- personal representatives for a deceased owner (e.g. executor or administrator of an estate);

EXAMPLE

Denis Dolan died in April 2013 leaving behind his own private residence and four residential properties, which he leased as short-term lettings. Under the terms of his will, the leased properties are left to his daughter and his former residence is left to his brother. Denis's solicitor and his nephew are appointed as the executors of Denis's estate.

The grant of probate finalising the administration of the estate issues in February 2014. As the estate is in administration on 1 May 2013 and 1 November 2013, the executors to Denis's estate are liable for LPT arising on the residential properties comprised in the estate. They must recover the cost of LPT from the estate as an expense of administration.

- trustees, where a property is held in a trust;

- local authorities or social housing organisations that own and provide social housing;

- where none of the above categories of liable person applies, the person who occupies the property on a rent-free basis and without challenge to that occupation is liable to LPT.

EXAMPLE

Nina Lowe died intestate on 11 March 2013. She was the sole registered owner of her house in Kilkenny, which she shared with her long-term partner Tim. Nina's next of kin are her sisters and brothers, who agreed to allow Tim continue living in the property until the letters of administration in respect of Nina's estate issued in February 2014. As Tim is living in the property on 1 May 2013 and 1 November 2013 and Nina died intestate, then Tim is liable for LPT arising for 2013 and 2014.

2.1.1 Co-ownership of a Property

Where co-ownership of a property arises, all owners will be held jointly and severally liable to LPT, but only one return will be required which will be submitted by the designated liable person.

"Joint and severally liable" means that each owner is individually liable or mutually liable for the full amount of LPT.

EXAMPLE

Ken Moore and Kevin Dunne purchased a number of residential properties under a co-ownership agreement. The properties are all leased under short-term lettings. Ken and Kevin have fallen out. LPT is due on all of the residential properties but Ken has left the country and Kevin has no way of contacting him. Kevin is willing to pay 50% of the LPT relating to his share. However, the Revenue Commissioners will hold the co-owner jointly and severally liable for the LPT and could therefore pursue Kevin for full payment.

2.1.2 Onus on a Taxpayer to Establish Liability

As LPT is a self-assessed tax, the onus is on the taxpayer to establish if he or she is the liable person. The presumption will usually be that the person who is occupying the property or who is the landlord of the property will be the liable person. While all owners of a jointly owned property are held to be jointly and severally liable for LPT, in the event of a dispute, it is the party who occupies the property who will be deemed to be the liable person *(section 12)*.

EXAMPLE

Mike and Marie are separated. Marie continues to live in the family home but both Mike and Marie are named on the deeds of the house. As they are both still owners of the residential property, then both are liable persons for the purpose of LPT. However, relations between Mike and Marie are very strained as Mike refuses to comply with a court order to support his and Marie's children and contribute towards the mortgage. Mike also refuses to pay the LPT due on the family home. Under section 12 of the Act, the liability to LPT will fall on to Marie as she is occupying the property.

2.1.3 Exemptions from LPT

There are no exemptions from LPT available to a liable person on financial grounds. However, LPT may be deferred if the liable person satisfies certain conditions as outlined in **Chapter 5**.

2.1.4 Companies

Finally, where the liable person is a company the LPT return must be prepared and filed by the company secretary *(section 35)*.

2.1.5 Difficulties in Establishing the Liable Person

In some instances, due perhaps to disputes or joint ownership, etc., it may be difficult to establish who is the liable person where there is no declaration. While Revenue have the power to specify who the designated liable person should be, the Act does state that the designated liable person shall be the *first* person to meet any of the conditions on the following list *(section 43)*:

- the person(s) elected by the other liable persons to be the designated liable person;

- the person who paid the 2012 Household Charge;

EXAMPLE

Kevin Murphy and James Molloy are co-owners of a rental property in Springfield, County Mayo. Kevin paid the household charge in respect of the property online in 2012 and James reimbursed Kevin in respect of his 50% share. As Kevin paid the household charge on Springfield, he will be treated as the designated liable person for LPT purposes in respect of this property.

- the person who paid the Non-principal Private Residence (NPPR) charge (where applicable);

- where a married couple or civil partners are jointly assessed (for tax purposes), and the property is jointly owned, the liable person is the assessable spouse or the nominated civil partner;

- if a property is owned by a partnership the precedent acting partner (i.e. the principal partner) is the liable person;

- where a property is owned jointly between a company and a person, it is the person who is liable;

- where a property is owned jointly between persons who are both resident and non-resident in the State, the liable person is the person who is resident or ordinarily resident in the State;

- the liable person is the person with the highest total income for tax purposes.

2.2 What is Liable to LPT?

A "relevant" residential property is liable to local property tax *(section 3)*. A residential property only becomes a "relevant" residential property if it is a residential property at the "liability" date.

EXAMPLE

Jack is planning some extensive remodelling to his house, which involves demolishing the property and rebuilding it. If Jack's house is demolished by 1 November 2013 with construction on the rebuild commencing on 2 November 2013, then he does not own a relevant property for the purpose of LPT for 2014.

A *residential property* means any building or structure (or part of a building) that is used as or is suitable for use as a dwelling, and includes any shed, outhouse, garage or other building or structure and grounds of up to one acre. The Act includes all privately owned property, properties owned by trusts, companies, partnerships, etc., and all residential properties owned by local authorities or approved housing bodies (subject to any exemption as set out in **Section 2.2.1**). Vacant properties are not exempt from LPT as they are "suitable for use" as a dwelling. It excludes a structure that is not permanently attached to the ground (e.g. caravan or mobile home).

EXAMPLE

Mary Murphy owns a two-acre site on which her dormer bungalow is located. Approximately one-third of an acre comprises the bungalow and a garden, the remainder being a horse paddock and horse shed. Though Mary's residential property is located on a two-acre site, only one acre of the land is to be included in the valuation of the residential property for the purposes of LPT. The horse shed is not enjoyed with the residential property and is excluded from the valuation.

2.2.1 Properties Exempt from Local Property Tax

It cannot be emphasised enough that there are no exemptions from local property tax for liable persons. However, in some cases certain **properties** may be exempt if the property satisfies one of the following categories of exemption:

Exemption Type	Details
A.	Any new, completed and previously unoccupied property, purchased from a builder/developer between 1 January 2013 and 31 October 2016, is exempt until the end of 2016 (*section 9*). This exemption only applies to the property and its first owner (but *note* that the first owner does not have to be a first-time buyer). If the property is sold during the exemption period, the new buyers cannot avail of the exemption.
B.	Any property purchased between 1 January 2013 and 31 December 2013 will be exempt until the end of 2016. (Due to a drafting error in the 'Act' this exemption applies to **all** buyers and not just first-time buyers as originally envisaged.) The property must be the person's sole or main residence, and if the property is subsequently sold or ceases to be the person's main residence between 2013 and 2016, the exemption no longer applies. *Note*: a buyer includes a property purchased by a married couple, civil partners or cohabitants so long as the property is their sole or main residence (*section 8*).

EXAMPLE

Civil partners Martin and Mark purchased their first home together in Portobello, Dublin in February 2013. Martin previously owned an apartment but the house in Portobello is Mark's first property purchase. The property will be exempt from LPT for 2013, 2014, 2015 and 2016 provided Martin and Mark continue to live in the house in Portobello as their only or main residence until 1 November 2015.

Exemption Type	Details
C.	Newly constructed properties are exempt from LPT but ONLY if each of the following four conditions are fulfilled (*section 6*): 1. the property must be constructed and owned by a builder or developer and is unsold; 2. the property must not as yet have been used as a residence; 3. the property must not have generated any taxable income for its owner; **and** 4. the property must have been treated in the accounts of the builder/developer as part of the stock in trade.

EXAMPLE

Dunphy Construction Ltd completed the development of a block of apartments in 2008. The development was undertaken as part of the company's trade of property construction for onward sale, but all the sales contracts on the apartments fell through with the collapse of the property market. In an effort to raise funds for loan repayments the company leased the apartments as short-term lettings in 2009 and the apartments have been occupied since that time. The properties continue to be reflected in the accounts of the company as trading stock.

Dunphy Construction Ltd's apartments will not qualify for the exemption from LPT as all four conditions under section 6 of the Act are not fulfilled, i.e. the apartments are occupied by tenants as dwellings and the apartments generated taxable income.

D.	Properties in unfinished housing estates (commonly called "ghost estates"), specified by the Minister for the Environment, Community and Local Government (*section 10*) and listed in the Finance (Local Property Tax) Regulations 2013 (S.I. No. 91 of 2013).

Exemption Type	Details
E.	Residential properties that have been certified by the Minister for the Environment, Community and Local Government as having significant pyritic damage will be exempt for a temporary period of approximately three years *(section 10A)*.

EXAMPLE

The Kenny family live in a house which has defects caused by pyrite damage. A certificate to this effect issues from the Department of Environment, Community and Local Government on 22 June 2014. The LPT exemption will apply for the liability dates on 1 November 2014 and 1 November 2015. As the certificate from the Department of Environment did not issue until 22 June 2014, the Kenny family must pay LPT for 2013 and 2014 by reference to the liability date 1 May 2013 and 1 November 2013.

However if the certificate is issued before 31 December 2013, the Kenny family can elect for either 1 May 2013 or 1 November 2013 to be treated as the first liability date and will therefore be entitled to an LPT exemption for three periods, i.e. either 2013, 2014 and 2015 (first liability date of 1 May 2013) or 2014, 2015 or 2016 (first liability date 1 November 2013).

F.	Residential properties owned by a charity or a public body and used to provide accommodation and support for people with special needs enabling them to live in the community (e.g. sheltered accommodation for the elderly or the disabled) *(section 7)*.

Exemption Type	Details
G.	Nursing Homes registered under the Health (Nursing Homes) Act 1990 (*section 5*).
H.	A property previously occupied by a person as their sole or main residence that has been vacated by the person for 12 months or more due to long-term mental or physical infirmity. An exemption may also be obtained, where the period is less than 12 months, if a doctor is satisfied that the person is unlikely, at any stage, to return to the property (*section 5*). In both cases, the exemption only applies where the property is not occupied by any other person. (**Note:** Where a property is owned by more than one person, the owners are jointly and severally liable for the payment of the tax and this exemption will not apply if the property in question is jointly owned with others.)
I.	A residential property purchased, built or adapted to make it suitable for occupation by a permanently and totally incapacitated individual as their sole or main residence, where an award has been made by the Personal Injuries Assessment Board or a court or where a trust has been established specifically for the benefit of such individuals. In the case of adaptations to a property, the exemption will only apply where the cost of the adaptations exceeds 25% of the market value of the property before it is adapted *(section 10B)*. The exemption ends if the property is sold and the incapacitated individual no longer occupies it as his or her sole or main residence.
J.	Mobile homes, vehicles or vessels (i.e. moveable).

Exemption Type	Details
K.	Properties fully subject to commercial rates (*section 4*). Where part of the property is used for commercial purposes (e.g. living accommodation over a shop), LPT is only due on the residential portion of the property. *Note:* even if the whole of a residential premises is used for commercial purposes (e.g. a guesthouse, B&B, etc.) LPT is only due where commercial rates are not paid.

EXAMPLE

Declan Murray owns a property which consists of a public house on the ground-floor level and his residential apartment on the second floor. He pays commercial property rates to Dublin City Council but qualifies for a mixed-domestic allowance. As the property is not fully subject to commercial rates, then LPT will apply to the property used as a residence.

EXAMPLE

Deirdre Shine owns and runs a B&B guesthouse. The property is also Deirdre's sole residence but she pays commercial rates on the whole property. The property will not be liable to LPT as the property is entirely used as a residence and is subject to commercial rates.

L.	Diplomatic properties.

Exemption Type	Details
M.	Properties used by charitable bodies as residential accommodation in connection with recreational activities that are an integral part of the body's charitable purpose, e.g. guiding and scouting activities (*section 7A*).

2.3 What is the Liability Date?

The liability date is quite important as it is the basis for the charge to local property tax.

If a property *is not* deemed to be a residential property at the liability date then no charge to LPT arises.

If a property *is* deemed to be a residential property at the liability date, then it becomes a "relevant" residential property and is liable to LPT.

The *liability date* is defined as:

- 1 May 2013, in respect of the year 2013; *and*

- in respect of any other year, 1 November in the preceding year (i.e. for 2014, the liability date is 1 November 2013; for 2015, the liability date is 1 November 2014, and so on).

A person who is the liable person of a residential property on 1 May 2013 is liable for LPT for 2013. If the liable person sells the residential property after 1 May 2013, but before 1 November 2013, he or she is still liable to LPT for 2013 but not for 2014. If the liable person sells the residential property after 1 November 2013, but before 31 December 2013, he or she is liable to LPT for 2013 and 2014 as he or she was the liable person at both liability dates.

2.4 What is the Valuation Date?

The valuation date should not be confused with the liability date, though the dates are similar. The liability date establishes that a property is a relevant residential property for the purposes of LPT. The *valuation date* is the date at which the chargeable value of the residential property for LPT is established. Section 13 of the Act states that this date is:

- 1 May 2013 for the tax years 2013, 2014, 2015 and 2016; *and*

- for each consecutive three-year period after 2016, 1 November in the preceding year (i.e. for 2017, the valuation date is 1 November 2016).

Any amendments to the value of the property after 1 May 2013, say, by way of extension, renovation, improvement or change of ownership of the property will not have any impact on the value of the property until the next valuation date of 1 November 2016.

EXAMPLE

The Byrne family home is valued at €220,000 on 1 May 2013. The Byrnes commence substantial renovations to their house on 2 May 2013 such that the house has a value of €350,000 on completion of the renovation work in October 2013. The LPT due by reference to the liability dates 1 May 2013, 1 November 2013, 1 November 2014 and 1 November 2015 is based on the value of the house on 1 May 2013 of €220,000 and does not have to be revised on foot of the increased value from the renovations completed in October 2013.

If a residential property is not a "relevant" residential property at 1 May 2013 and therefore has no value at the valuation date of 1 May 2013, the property is not liable to LPT until the next valuation date of 1 November 2016, i.e. there is no liability to LPT until 2017 (*section 14*).

2.4.1 *Change of Ownership between Valuation Dates*

Where there is a change of ownership or other event (such as the granting of a long-term lease) which results in a change to the liable person, the details of the current value for LPT purposes must be passed on to the new liable person either by informing them as to what chargeable value/valuation band was used at the last valuation date or by providing a copy of the LPT return (*section 14*).

However, the Act does confer a requirement on any new liable person to decide whether the previous liable person could "reasonably" have arrived at the chargeable value that was returned in respect of the last valuation date (*section 35*). "Reasonably" is not defined but the Revenue Commissioner's own guidelines would indicate that any new liable person will have to 'work backwards' from the selling price to see if any intervening factors since the last valuation date could account for the uplift in the property's value. Examples would include the addition of an extension to the property or the announcement of a new rail link to the area since the last valuation date.

Where the new liable person forms the view that the chargeable value that was declared by the previous owner was too low, he or she is required to submit a revised chargeable value in relation to the liability date following a sale (*section 35*). Where a purchaser forms the view that the property had not been undervalued, he or she can continue to rely on the vendor's valuation until the next valuation date without submitting a revised return.

3

Calculating Local Property Tax

3.1 Establishing the "Chargeable Value" of a Residential Property

LPT is a self-assessed tax, which means that the liable person is obliged to determine the chargeable value of the relevant residential property and to pay the tax due based on that valuation. This sounds simple, but many taxpayers, particularly those new to the operation of a self-assessed tax, will struggle with the notion of having to calculate and pay the tax due. Furthermore, all taxpayers will, in a stagnant housing market, struggle to establish a market value for any property.

However, the Act does recognise the difficulties that valuation may create for some taxpayers and requires the Revenue Commissioners to provide and publish guidelines in relation to the matter of ascertaining the chargeable value of relevant residential properties (*section 15*). The Act also states that a liable person who makes a self-assessment based on these Revenue guidelines and pays the amount of the self-assessment will not be challenged by Revenue on that assessment. (*Note*: This section does not apply to any property with a value in excess of €1 million.)

3.1.1 Problems in Establishing Chargeable Value

Outside of the difficulty of estimating a market value for a residential property in the current economic climate, many properties have specific characteristics that may make them more difficult to value. For example, issues with:

- access to a property (e.g. a farmhouse accessible only through a farmyard);
- a property that is part of another property (e.g. a 'granny' flat);
- a property in 'negative' equity;
- a property modified for a disabled person, etc.;

will increase the difficulties in estimating the market value of a property.

The Act is quite specific under its definition of "chargeable value" (*section 2*) that the *value*:

- is that which the property might reasonably be expected to fetch from an open market sale and is the best price that could be achieved for the vendor;
- is the unencumbered value (i.e. before any mortgage or debt);
- ignores any issue relating to access, in that it assumes that the same access rights that existed before the sale remain in place.

EXAMPLE

Colin Jones lives in a house on his parents' farm. He has a mortgage of €50,000 on the house. His house is only accessible by driving through the farmyard. The market value of the house taking the farmyard access into account is €140,000, whereas the market value of the house ignoring the farmyard access is €210,000. What is the chargeable value of the property for the purposes of the local property tax?

The mortgage of €50,000 is disregarded for the purpose of arriving at the chargeable value. The fact that the house is only accessible through a farmyard owned by Colin's parents is also ignored and the chargeable value for LPT is €210,000.

EXAMPLE

Gretta White lives in a self-contained flat attached to her son Henry's house. While Henry is the legal owner of the house Gretta has a right of residence in the flat.

In this case Henry is the liable person for the house excluding the flat and Gretta is the liable person for the flat.

If Henry were the liable person for both properties he has the option of valuing both properties separately or of valuing the granny flat as part of the overall building.

Property Modified for a Disabled Person

There is some relief available on the chargeable value where a property was adapted for use by a disabled person and the adaptations have increased the value of the property *(section 15A)*.

The chargeable value of the property may be reduced by the lesser of:

- the maximum grant payable (not necessarily paid) under the relevant local authority scheme (Housing (Adaptation Grants for Older People and People with a Disability) Regulations 2007 (S.I. No. 670 of 2007), or under regulation 4 of the Housing (Disabled Persons and Essential Repairs Grants) Regulations 2001 (S.I. No. 607 of 2001);

or

- by the amount of the increase in the property's value that is attributable to the work carried out, ***provided*** the person with the disability occupies the property as his or her sole or main residence.

EXAMPLE

John Brophy is disabled and lives full-time in a 20-year-old property with a chargeable value of €320,000. Following a stroke in 2012, John's home was modified to enable him to continue living there. He received grant aid from the local council of €20,000 out of a maximum available grant of €24,000. He estimates that the modifications increased the market value of his home by €30,000.

Value of property	€320,000
Less: Maximum grant payable	€(24,000)
Chargeable Value for LPT	€296,000

3.1.2 Sources of Information for Valuing a Property

Revenue Guidelines

The Revenue Commissioners (www.revenue.ie) provide an online interactive guide, which lists average market values of properties in a given locality depending on age and type. Revenue does not, however, provide market values for individual properties. They state that the guidance is primarily based on the market value of properties in the area that were sold since the year 2010, with some adjustment for price movements in the interim. The valuation guidance is based on:

- The type of property split into the following categories:
  - apartment/flat,
  - bungalow,
  - detached, semi-detached or terraced.
- The average price of the type of property for the general area.
- The age of the property, e.g. built before the year 2000 or after.

Revenue, however, is very clear that if the liable property has specific features that would render it outside the average value of properties in the locality the liable person has to factor these in when valuing the property.

For example, if the average value for a detached house in the local area is given on Revenue's interactive guide as €300,000 but the liable person owns a detached house of 20,000 square feet where the local average square footage is 2,000 square feet, then the liable person cannot rely on the Revenue guide as a basis for valuation.

Register of Residential Property Sales
The register of residential property sales, published by the Property Services Regulatory Authority (PSRA) (www.propertypriceregister. ie), is based on Revenue stamp duty data. New property prices are shown exclusive of VAT at 13.5% and any property not sold at full market price is also highlighted (though the reason why the sale was not for full market value is not given). In determining the relevant valuation band for a residential property, the VAT-inclusive price must be taken into account.

Professional Valuation
A taxpayer, or a group of taxpayers, may choose to employ a professional valuer/auctioneer to value a single or group of properties in an area or estate. Also, if a taxpayer purchased a property or obtained a professional valuation in recent years, this valuation may be used if adjusted for any change in property values in the area or in the value of the individual property (by way of improvement or alteration, etc.) since the date of this valuation.

Irrespective of the source of information used to value a residential property (which the liable person should retain as evidence of the basis used), the onus remains on the liable person to calculate the chargeable value of a relevant residential property.

3.1.3 Valuing a Property

Thus, on the one hand, the liable person is being told that if he or she follows Revenue's valuation guidelines 'honestly', Revenue will accept the property value assessment and, on the other hand, that if the liable person feels that the guidance does not indicate a reasonable valuation for the property, the liable person should make his or her own assessment. This brings the liable person back to the same question: "How do I value my property?"

The first thing to remember is that, for properties under €1 million, the valuation does not have to be an exact sum. The property value will fall within a specific valuation band, which begins at €0 to €100,000 and increases in increments of €50,000 thereafter until the top valuation band of €1 million. Therefore, the valuation has to be to the nearest €50,000.

The following steps should be taken when assessing the value of a property:

Step 1: Check the guideline value for the residential property from Revenue's website.

Step 2: The liable person should ask themselves: "Is my house indicative of the same category houses in the area?" For example, is the property roughly the same as the Browns' house, the Smiths' house and the O'Sullivans' house on the road? If your answer is "yes" it would appear it is safe to rely on the Revenue guideline figure.

Step 3: If your answer is "no", then consider the following:

- What is the estimated value of the difference between your house and the same category houses in the area? For example, if the only difference between you and your neighbours is a designer landscaped garden or a new sun-room is this likely to push the value of your home up by €50,000 to the next valuation band?

- Is your house a one-off and considerably bigger/smaller than the same category houses in the area?
- Is your site (up to a maximum of one acre) larger/smaller than the same category houses in the area?
- Do you have extensive out-buildings/yards (non-commercial and within the one acre) that would increase the value of your property by an additional €50,000?
- Is your apartment a three-bedroom penthouse, whereas the majority in the area are one-bedroom or studio apartments?

By working through the different steps, the liable person should probably be able to establish a broad valuation for their property; however, they should always keep some documentary evidence or note of how the valuation was arrived at should Revenue query the valuation.

For properties with a value in excess of €1 million, the chargeable value must be an exact valuation, i.e. it cannot fall within a valuation 'band'. It is advisable for the liable person to get a professional valuation of the property as the protection afforded to the taxpayer under section 15 of the Act, where the liable person follows the Revenue guidelines when valuing a property, does not apply where the value of the property is in excess of €1 million. If the property or a similar property was bought or sold in recent times, the market value could be used as a guide to establishing the chargeable value. In all cases, care should be taken to keep any relevant documentation or information in support of the estimated value.

3.2 How to Calculate Local Property Tax

Once the value of the residential property is established, the calculation of LPT is very straightforward. Property values are organised into valuation bands and LPT is calculated at:

- **0.18%** per annum on the mid-point of the valuation band into which the property falls, **up to €1 million; and**

- **0.25%** per annum on the portion of the property value **exceeding €1 million**.

The **valuation bands** are as follows:

Valuation Band Number	Valuation Band €	Mid-point of Valuation Band €	LPT in 2013 (half-year charge) €	LPT in 2014, 2015, 2016 (full-year charge) €
01	0 to 100,000	50,000	45	90
02	100,001 to 150,000	125,000	112	225
03	150,001 to 200,000	175,000	157	315
04	200,001 to 250,000	225,000	202	405
05	250,001 to 300,000	275,000	247	495
06	300,001 to 350,000	325,000	292	585
07	350,001 to 400,000	375,000	337	675
08	400,001 to 450,000	425,000	382	765
09	450,001 to 500,000	475,000	427	855
10	500,001 to 550,000	525,000	472	945
11	550,001 to 600,000	575,000	517	1,035
12	600,001 to 650,000	625,000	562	1,125
13	650,001 to 700,000	675,000	607	1,215

(See overleaf for Band Nos. 14–19.)

(Valuation Bands–Continued)

Valuation Band Number	Valuation Band	Mid-point of Valuation Band	LPT in 2013 (half-year charge)	LPT in 2014, 2015, 2016 (full-year charge)
14	700,001 to 750,000	725,000	652	1,305
15	750,001 to 800,000	775,000	697	1,395
16	800,001 to 850,000	825,000	742	1,485
17	850,001 to 900,000	875,000	787	1,575
18	900,001 to 950,000	925,000	832	1,665
19	950,001 to 1,000,000*	975,000	877	1,755

* Residential properties valued **over €1 million** will be assessed at the actual value at **0.18%** on the first €1 million in value and **0.25%** on the portion of the value above €1 million (no banding will apply).

EXAMPLE

John Draper's residential property has a market value of
€330,000 as of 1 May 2013. John's liability to LPT is as
follows:

Market Value	€330,000
Valuation Band Number	06
Valuation Band	€300,000 to €350,000
Mid-point of Valuation Band	**€325,000**

LPT:

€325,000 @ 0.18%	€585
LPT 2013 (50%)	€292
LPT 2014, 2015, 2016	€585

EXAMPLE

Betty Ryan's residential property has been valued by an auctioneer as having a market value of €1,300,000 as of 1 May
2013. Her liability to LPT is as follows:

LPT:

€1,000,000 @ 0.18%	€1,800
€300,000 @ 0.25%	€750
Total	€2,550

LPT 2013 (50%)	€1,275
LPT 2014, 2015, 2016	€2,550

Multiple Properties

Where a liable person has multiple properties, each property
is individually valued and LPT calculated thereon (*section 18*).
The liable person's liability to LPT is the cumulative of the
individual LPT due on each property rather than a percentage of

the cumulative value of the property portfolio. For example, three properties each valued at €500,000 are charged individually to LPT using the valuation bands with a total annual liability of €2,565 (Band 09, €855 × 3). The calculation is not on an aggregate value of €1.5 million, which would give a liability of €3,050.

4

Returns, Payments and Payment Options

4.1 Local Property Tax Returns

The obligation to submit an unprompted tax return is not a new concept for those who are self-employed and therefore self-assessed, but it can be a difficult concept for many other categories of taxpayer who usually pay taxes by way of deduction (e.g. PAYE, VAT, etc.). With self-assessment the onus is on the taxpayer to both declare and pay any taxes due – the taxpayer cannot wait for the Revenue Commissioners to contact them, they must contact Revenue. So it is with the local property tax. While Revenue issued local property tax returns (Form LPT1) to the majority of residential property owners in early 2013, which included a Revenue estimate of the LPT payable, the onus remains on the liable person to file an LPT return (*section 28*).

4.1.1 *What Happens if you Receive an LPT Return from the Revenue?*

- If you are the liable person of the residential property, you must make a return confirming that you are the liable person of that residential property. You must determine the market value of the residential property, calculate the tax due thereon and specify one of the payment options as listed on the return.
- If you are not the liable person you must contact Revenue within 30 days of receipt of the return, and explain why you are not the liable person, providing some documentation, if available, to support your assertion (e.g. a copy of a lease agreement, etc.) and let Revenue know who the liable person is, if known (*section 34*).
- If you are the liable person and wish to claim an exemption, the return must be completed and filed by the relevant

deadline and you must state in the return which exemption condition the property satisfies (e.g. first-time buyer, 'ghost estate', etc.) by reference to the exemption type: A, B, C, etc. (see **Chapter 2**).

- If you are the liable person and wish to claim a deferral (full or partial) (see **Chapter 5**) the return must be completed and filed by the relevant deadlines and you must state in the return which deferral exemption is being claimed.

Doing nothing is not an option.

4.1.2 What if you Don't Receive an LPT Return from Revenue?

- If you have a residential property and are a liable person in respect of that property, you are obliged to contact Revenue either to request an LPT return, or to make an LPT return on-line.
- Owners of multiple properties will not receive a return from Revenue but are obliged to file a return and pay LPT online.
- ROS (the 'Revenue On-Line Service') customers will also not receive a return from Revenue but will too have to file and pay LPT online.

Again, if you are a liable person, doing nothing is not an option.

4.1.3 The Register

The Act imposed a requirement on Revenue to compile and maintain a register of residential properties, along with an associated list of the liable person in respect of each property (*section 27*).

In the first instance, Revenue compiled a register from numerous sources including utility companies (Electric Ireland, Telecom, Bord Gáis, etc.), the Household Charge Register and the Private Residential Tenancies Board (PRTB) in an effort to establish the correct liable person for each property. Based on this data and on its own records, Revenue then sent letters to those who it had reason to believe were liable persons. For example, in situations where a landlord had not registered with the PRTB, or where a tenant rather than the owner was registered with a utility company, a tenant might have been identified as the liable person.

There are probably instances where a return was issued to the wrong person; to a deceased person; in respect of a property which is not a residential property; even where duplicate returns for the same property were issued. However, in any scenario where correspondence is received from Revenue it should never be ignored and the person in receipt of such correspondence should contact Revenue to clarify/correct the draft register.

Finally, it is worth noting that a liable person can have their LPT return made on their behalf and under their authority by another person (e.g. a relative). However, the liable person is still responsible and accountable for the return made under their authority (*section 36*).

4.2 Local Property Tax – Return Filing Dates

The due date for submitting any tax return is an important date as it is from this date that a person is deemed to be in default where a return is filed late, is incomplete (e.g. no payment either enclosed or payment method stipulated) or not filed at all. Where returns are filed electronically Revenue's practice has been to give an extended period for filing so long as the return is filed completely and payment made or payment method stipulated by the extended filing date. However, in all cases (even if an incomplete return is filed by the electronic filing due date) the due date is the earlier date and interest and penalties are calculated from that date in the event of a default.

A liable person is obliged to file their LPT return by the following due dates:

1. **For liability date 1 May 2013 (for years 2013, 2014, 2015 and 2016):**

   - **7 May 2013** – due date for filing LPT return.

   This due date was extended to **28 May 2013** where the LPT return was filed electronically.

   Once a return was made for the liability date 1 May 2013, this return remains valid for tax years 2013 (half year) 2014, 2015 and 2016 provided LPT is paid in respect of each year.

2. For liability date 1 November 2016 (for year 2017 *et seq.*):

- **7 November 2016** – due date for filing LPT return

(*Note:* while not stated in the Act, it is envisaged that an extension to the filing dates will be given for returns filed electronically in 2016, 2017 *et seq.*)

Where a claim is made for a deferral (see **Chapter 5**), a return has to be filed every year, i.e. by 7 May 2013 for 2013; 7 November 2013 for 2014; 7 November 2014 for tax year 2015, and so on (*section 35*).

4.3 Change of Ownership

4.3.1 *Continuation of Chargeable Value until the Next Valuation Date*

Where there is a change of ownership of a residential property between valuation dates (i.e. the date upon which the chargeable value of the property is established, e.g. 1 May 2013; 1 November 2016) the new owner can continue to use the chargeable value set at the previous valuation date until the next valuation date (subject to the exception outlined at **Section 4.3.3**). The previous owner must give the new owner details of the chargeable value returned for LPT purposes and/or a copy of the LPT return.

EXAMPLE

Patricia Jayne purchased a house from John Ryan on 24 June 2014 for €310,000. John produced a copy of his LPT return for 2013 where the chargeable value was declared to be in valuation band 5 (between €250,000 and €300,000). While the sale price is in the higher band 6 (between €300,000 and €350,000), the band 5 value will continue to be used until the next valuation date on 1 November 2016.

This rule also applies where the property was not a relevant residential property at the previous valuation date and consequently did not have a chargeable value at that date.

EXAMPLE

John Ryan owned a ruin which was not a residential property on 1 May 2013 and consequently did not have a chargeable value at the valuation date of 1 May 2013. John commenced work on restoring and extending the ruin in September 2013 and sold the resulting house to Patricia Jayne in June 2014 for €250,000. This new property is not taxable until the next valuation date, which is 1 November 2016, as it did not have a chargeable value at 1 May 2013. Thus, no liability to LPT exists until the tax year 2017.

4.3.2 Sale/Transfer of an Exempt Property

Where a property is purchased/transferred from a person who qualified for **Exemption Type B** (see **Section 2.2.1**), i.e. the property was purchased in the **year 2013** and used as the person's sole or main residence, the new owner must make a return for the first liability date after the transfer of ownership of the property. The new owner must estimate what the chargeable value of the property would have been at the previous valuation date and pay the tax due based thereon.

However, if the new owner also purchased the property in the **year 2013** and uses the property as his sole or main residence, he is also entitled to claim an exemption from LPT under Exemption Type B.

EXAMPLE

Margo Healy purchased her home in March 2013 and claimed Exemption B in her LPT return, which she submitted on 3 May 2013. In June 2014, Margo sold her house for €325,000 to Joan Bruton, who does not qualify for the first-time buyer exemption. As Margo is the liable person for the house for 2013 and 2014, Joan will only be required to pay LPT for 2015 onwards. At the liability date of 1 November 2014, Joan must estimate what the value of the house was at the previous

31

valuation date of 1 May 2013. As the estate agent and newspaper articles contend that there has been a general upswing in property prices in the area of 10%, Joan can safely value her house at €295,000 (band 5) and pay LPT of €495 for each of the years 2015 and 2016.

4.3.3 Obligations of New Owners

The Act imposes a rather hefty obligation on a new owner to effectively 'audit' the chargeable value at the previous valuation date as supplied by the old owner (*section 35*). The new owner is required to form an opinion as to whether this chargeable value is one that "could reasonably have been arrived at". This would only appear to arise where the purchase price paid by the new owner is significantly higher than the chargeable value supplied by the previous owner. Where the new owner is of the opinion that the chargeable value was undervalued by the previous owner, the new owner is obliged to submit an LPT return in respect of the next liability date showing a revised chargeable value for the property at the previous valuation date.

EXAMPLE

Tomás Breen bought a residential property for €310,000 from Francis Roche in March 2014. During the purchase process, Francis supplied Tomás with a copy of his LPT return, which showed the property in valuation band 3 (€150,001–€200,000). Francis is unable to provide any reason why the value of the property has increased so much in the 11 months, and as Tomás is unaware of any valid reason for such an increase in market value other than a general increase of 10% in property values in the area, he is obliged to submit an LPT return in respect of 1 November 2014 showing a revised valuation band for the property at the previous valuation date of 1 May 2013. Tomás returns valuation band 5 (€250,000–€300,000) to take into account the general uplift in values of 10% from 1 May 2013 as follows:

Sale price	€310,000
Less: 10% "uplift"	€(28,182)
Value at 1/5/2013	€281,818

Revenue is at pains to point out that this requirement does not oblige new owners to make their own valuation of a property in all cases but merely to decide whether the valuation that was returned could have been reasonably arrived at. Of course, one person's reasonableness may be another's stubbornness! However, there are some obvious reasons why a property's value could have significantly increased from the last valuation date, e.g. significant repairs and improvements to the property thereby increasing its value; announcement of a new rail link to the area, etc. Nevertheless, the onus remains on the new owner to satisfy himself as to the reasonableness of the valuation and while the previous owner may supply supporting evidence for the increase in value, it is the new owner who is obliged to make the LPT return with the revised valuation figure.

Self-correction by the Previous Owner

Where in the course of the sale/transfer of a property the old owner considers that their valuation at the previous valuation date was conservative or possibly undervalued, they can make a self-correction by submitting a revised LPT return with the revised valuation band and pay the additional LPT liability. The old owner must inform the new owner of the revision to the chargeable value as a revised chargeable value displaces the previous valuation. Even in the case of a self-correction and a revised valuation, the onus still remains on the new owner to consider if the new valuation was reasonably arrived at.

4.4 Payment of Local Property Tax

Local property tax liabilities can be paid in one single payment or phased out into equal instalments from 1 July 2013 until the end of the year. The payment method selected for 2013 will automatically apply for 2014 (effective from 1 January 2014) and subsequent years unless the Revenue Commissioners are otherwise advised.

LPT can be paid in full in **one payment** by:

- Single Debit Authority – this authorises payment of LPT in one deduction from an account in a bank or other financial institution. This authority can only be used once and while an LPT return is not required every year the taxpayer will have to inform Revenue each year of his or her bank account details in order to pay LPT each year by single debit authority. Customers should take care to quote the correct account number. The single debit authority only works for Irish financial institutions (including credit unions) and not foreign bank accounts or credit card accounts.
- Cheque or debit/credit card (payment is taken at date of instruction).
- Cash payment (including debit/credit card) through approved payment service providers (e.g. An Post/Postpoint, Omnivend or Payzone).

LPT can be paid, on a **phased basis**, from 1 July 2013 by:

- Deduction at source from salary or occupational pension.
- Deduction at source from certain payments received from the Department of Social Protection (though the deduction cannot reduce the DSP personal rate payment to less than €186 per week).
- Deduction at source from scheme payments received from the Department of Agriculture, Food and the Marine.
- Direct debit.
- Cash payments (including debit/credit card) through approved payment service providers (e.g. An Post/Postpoint, Omnivend or Payzone).

> *Note*: the Act allows for another person to pay LPT on behalf of a liable person, for example, a daughter paying the tax on behalf of her father (*section 16*). This is an important concession as the payment of LPT by one individual on behalf of another will not be treated as a gift or an income payment for the purposes of other taxes and so can be made without any further liability to tax.

4.4.1 *Voluntary Deduction of Local Property Tax from Salaries/Pensions*

Employers (including pension providers) are required to make phased payment options available to those employees who wish to pay their LPT as a deduction at source from their net salary/pension.

Where this payment option is chosen by the liable person, Revenue will have notified the employer on the employer tax credit certificate (P2C) of the amount of LPT to be deducted evenly over the pay periods between 1 July and 31 December 2013. This payment method automatically applies for 2014 and subsequent years unless the employee contacts Revenue and confirms an alternative payment option, in which case Revenue will contact the employer to cease the deductions from salary. The employer is required to account for and remit the LPT along with PAYE, PRSI and USC.

Where the deduction at source option is chosen by the liable person, Revenue will advise the employer, pension provider or the relevant government department of the amount to be deducted. Interest does not apply to phased payments.

LPT can only be deducted where the employer has received an employer tax credit certificate (P2C) showing the amount of LPT to be deducted and the employer can only cease deduction of LPT from net salary when advised to do so by Revenue, i.e. the employee cannot direct the employer to amend, commence or cancel collection of LPT.

Similarly, any queries, questions or disputes regarding LPT amounts or property valuations are a matter between the employee and the Revenue Commissioners.

The following is an extract from an employer tax credit certificate (P2C) showing USC rates and LPT deduction:

Universal Social Charge (USC)					
Rates of USC			Exemption Case **N**		
USC Rate 1	2%		**Yearly COP**	**Monthly COP**	**Weekly COP**
USC Rate 2	4%	**USC Rate 1 Cut-Off Point**	11,000.00	916.67	211.54
USC Rate 3	7%	**USC Rate 2 Cut-Off Point**	15,000.00	1,250.00	288.47

The following details of Gross Pay for USC purposes and USC deduction, from 1 January 2013, to date of commencement with your employment, should be taken into account when calculating current USC deductions.

Total Gross Pay
for USC purposes: 0.00   **Total USC deducted:**   0.00

Local Property Tax (LPT)

Total LPT to be deducted: **260.00**

Under the LPT heading,

- where deduction at source does not apply or is to stop, LPT will be shown as €0.00,
- where deduction at source applies, a figure for LPT will be shown.

LPT deductions are spread out evenly over the number of pay periods left in the year from the time Revenue informs the employer. For example, if an employee is paid weekly and has an LPT liability of €350 for 2014 and Revenue informs the employer of this amount after the second pay period, the LPT amount is deducted evenly over the remaining 50 pay periods (€350 ÷ 50 = €7 per pay period).

LPT deductions are from an employee's net salary (i.e. after deducting PAYE/PRSI/USC and allowable pension contributions) but take priority over non-statutory deductions and any deductions under a Court Order where the Court Order was made after 30 June 2013.

At the end of the tax year, the employee's P60 certificate will show the total amount of LPT deducted by the employer/pension provider in that year. If an employee changes employer during the year, the previous employer will record the total amount of LPT deducted on the employee's Form P45, which Revenue will use to inform the new employer of the amount of LPT to be deducted thereafter.

4.4.2 *Voluntary Deduction of Local Property Tax from Department of Social Protection Payments*

A liable person in receipt of payments from the Department of Social Protection (DSP) can elect to have LPT deducted from DSP payments provided the deduction does not reduce the liable person's DSP personal rate payment to less than €186 per week. While LPT payments can be deducted, in theory, from all schemes as specified in sections 39 and 139 of the Social Welfare Consolidation Act 2005 (*section 83 of the Act*), in practice, LPT will be deducted from the following DSP payments:

- state pension (contributory);
- state pension (non-contributory);
- widow/widower/surviving civil partner's contributory pension;
- widow/widower/surviving civil partner's non-contributory pension;

- state pension (transition);
- one-parent family payment;
- invalidity pension;
- carer's allowance;
- disability allowance;
- blind pension.

The onus is on the liable person, when submitting their LPT return and specifying the DSP payment option, to ensure that the payment of LPT does not reduce the DSP rate to less than €186 per week. If it will do so, the liable person must make alternative arrangements for the payment of the full amount of LPT due, i.e. a portion cannot come from the DSP payment and a portion in cash. Neither can the LPT deduction be taken from two separate DSP payment schemes (e.g. split between a married couple's individual DSP payments). Only one payment method is allowed for the full payment of LPT. The Department of Social Protection is obliged to return any amount of LPT deducted to the Revenue Commissioners within seven days from the date of making the payment.

4.4.3 *Voluntary Deduction of Local Property Tax from Department of Agriculture Payments*

A liable person in receipt of payments from the Department of Agriculture, Food and the Marine (DAFM) can elect to have LPT deducted from DAFM payments. The list of payments from which LPT at source may be deducted is derived from the Agriculture Appeals Act 2001, and includes:

- Beef Cow Scheme in Less Severely Handicapped Areas and Coastal Areas with Specific Handicaps;
- Cattle Headage Scheme in More Severely Handicapped Areas;
- Equine Headage Scheme in all Disadvantaged Areas;
- EU Area Aid Scheme (including the Arable Aid Scheme);
- EU De-seasonalisation Slaughter Premium Scheme;
- EU Ewe Premium Scheme;
- EU Extensification Premium Scheme;
- EU Slaughter Premium Scheme;
- EU Special Beef Premium Scheme;
- EU Suckler Cow Premium Scheme;
- Farm Improvement Programme (FIP);

- Farm Improvement Programme (FIP) Horticulture;
- Goat Headage Scheme in all Disadvantaged Areas;
- Installation Aid Scheme (IAS);
- National Scheme of Installation Aid (SIA) (introduced December 1998);
- National Scheme of Investment Aid for the Control of Farm Pollution (introduced June 1999);
- National Scheme of Investment Aid for the Improvement of Dairy Hygiene Standards (introduced May 1999);
- Non-valuation aspects of the On-Farm Valuation Scheme for TB and Brucellosis Reactors;
- Rural Environment Protection Scheme (REPS);
- Scheme of Early Retirement from Farming;
- Scheme of Grant-Aid for Investment in Alternative Enterprises;
- Scheme of Grant-Aid for Investments in Agri-Tourism;
- Scheme of Installation Aid (SIA);
- Scheme of Investment Aid for Farm Waste Management (FWM);
- Scheme of Investment Aid for the Control of Farm Pollution (CFP);
- Scheme of Investment Aid for the Improvement of Dairy Hygiene Standards (DHS);
- Scheme of Investment Aid for Upgrading of On-farm Dairying Facilities;
- Scheme of Investment Aid in Alternative Enterprises (Housing and Handling Facilities) (AES);
- Sheep Headage Scheme in all Disadvantaged Areas.

While the Revenue Commissioners and the Department of Social Welfare share a unique identifier, i.e. the personal public service number (PPSN) of the liable person, this is not the case with the Department of Agriculture, Food and the Marine. Accordingly, when a liable person is opting to have LPT withheld from DAFM payments, they must either provide their herd number, or, in the case of retirement scheme payments, the registration number.

As with **Section 4.4.2** above, the onus is on the liable person when submitting their LPT return and specifying the DAFM payment option, to ensure that the DAFM payment is sufficient to allow full payment of LPT due. If not, the liable person must make alternative arrangements for the payment of the full amount of LPT due, i.e. a portion cannot come from the DAFM and another source. Only one payment method is allowed for the full payment of LPT.

4.4.4 Obligations of Employers and Pension Providers in Administrating Voluntary Deduction of Local Property Tax

Where the option for a voluntary deduction from salary or pension payments is chosen by the liable person, employers and pension providers are obliged to make this facility available from July 2013 onwards. The Revenue Commissioners will issue a revised employer tax credit certificate (P2C) showing the amount of LPT to be deducted, which the employer/pension provider will deduct in even amounts over the remaining number of pay dates in the year.

A liable person cannot request an employer/pension provider to either increase, decrease, cease or commence an LPT payment amount: any amendments to the LPT amounts must be communicated to the employer/pension provider only by Revenue.

EXAMPLE

Nora Watts is employed by Bulbs Ltd and has elected to have her LPT liability of €230 for 2013 deducted from her monthly salary over the six-month period 1 July to 31 December. Bulbs Ltd did not receive a revised P2C for Nora until 31 July 2013, when the July payroll had already been run and paid. From 1 August to 31 December, Bulbs Ltd will deduct €46 per month (€230 ÷ 5) from Nora's monthly salary. There is no necessity for a revision of the July payroll.

The employer/pension provider will return the LPT deducted to Revenue along with the PAYE/PRSI/USC on the monthly P30 returns, by the 23rd of the month immediately following the income tax month, and will account for the cumulative amounts in the P35/35L year-end returns. Cumulative amounts of LPT deducted will also be shown on the employee's annual P60 or a P45 if the employee leaves.

LPT cannot be deducted from other non-salary/pension payments (e.g. refund of expenses) and are not deducted on a cumulative basis.

Order of Deductions where a Court Order is in place BEFORE an Original P2C is Issued

The priority of the deduction of LPT in relation to PAYE/PRSI/USC deductions under Court Orders and non-statutory deductions is as follows:

1. PAYE/PSRI/USC and allowable pension contributions;
2. Court Order;
3. LPT;
4. non-statutory deductions (e.g. union subscriptions, savings schemes, etc.).

Order of Deductions where a Court Order is put in place AFTER an Original P2C is Issued:

1. PAYE/PSRI/USC and allowable pension contributions;
2. LPT;
3. Court Order;
4. non-statutory deductions (e.g. union subscriptions, savings schemes, etc.).

Insufficient Salary Amounts

Where there is a shortfall in LPT collected due to an insufficient net salary amount in a particular pay period (say, for example, due to extended sick leave, unpaid time off, etc.), the employer/pension provider must adjust the amount of LPT to be deducted for the remaining pay periods in the year to ensure that the full amount of LPT is collected. If this is done, and the full amount of LPT is collected/collectible by the year end, the employer/pension provider is not required to notify the Revenue Commissioners. However, if, based on the expected income of the employee for the remainder of the year, the employee will not have sufficient income to satisfy their full LPT liability, the employer/pension provider must notify Revenue in writing about the expected shortfall.

Protection for Employers/Pension Providers

The Act offers protection for employers and pension providers operating the LPT deduction scheme whereby the employer/pension provider is indemnified against any claim by an employee that the employer/pension provider underpaid an employee by virtue of the deduction of LPT as authorised by Revenue (*section 82*).

4.5 Overpayment/Refunds of Local Property Tax

Where an overpayment of LPT was due to an error or a mistake in the LPT return, a claim for a repayment may be made by the taxpayer provided (*section 26*);

- the claim is made within four years after the end of the year in which the liability date fell;
- a true and complete LPT return has been prepared and filed; and
- any information sought by Revenue in relation to the claim has been supplied.

EXAMPLE

Sheila Maguire submitted an LPT return and paid the LPT in respect of her residence for 2013. As Sheila was actually in full-time residential care for the elderly since December 2011, the property was exempt for LPT purposes in 2013 and subsequent years as Sheila continued in long-term care. Sheila can make a claim for a refund of the LPT paid but she must do so before 31 December 2017 for LPT she paid in respect of the liability date of 1 May 2013 and 1 November 2013.

Where a liable person has over- or underpaid LPT and is paying LPT by voluntary deduction (i.e. from salaries/pensions, DSP or DAFM payments), the obligation is on the liable person to contact Revenue to rectify any over- or underpayment. The employer/pension provider, DSP or DAFM are not allowed to make any refunds of LPT.

5

Deferral of Local Property Tax

5.1 Overview

The introduction of the local property tax (LPT) broke one of the 'sacred' rules implicit within the Irish tax system. Up to its introduction, the notion of "ability to pay" has nearly always been a factor in the design and implementation of taxes. The previous residential property tax (RPT) was based on property value **AND** an income threshold limit, and the 2012 Household Charge had more exemptions on income grounds than a sieve has holes. LPT is different – if you own or have an exclusive right of residence in a relevant residential property you are liable to LPT, irrespective of your ability to pay.

Though there are circumstances in which the liability to LPT can be fully or partially **deferred** to a later date, it must be emphasised that deferral is **not an exemption**, merely a deferral of the payment of the tax (plus interest) until a later date. The deferred tax along with interest at 4% per annum remains a charge on the property and will have to be paid to Revenue when the property is sold. Where a property is transferred, by way of gift or inheritance, to another person, the LPT also becomes payable at the transfer date unless the new liable person too qualifies for a deferral.

There are four circumstances in which a deferral or partial deferral of LPT is available:

1. income threshold (see **Section 5.2**);
2. personal representative of a deceased person (see **Section 5.3**);
3. personal insolvency (see **Section 5.4**); and
4. hardship (see **Section 5.5**).

Deferral options 1, 2 and 3 are all accepted on a self-assessment basis, i.e. the liable person makes the claim which is accepted by Revenue. However, if the liable person is found to have used false or inaccurate information to secure a deferral of LPT, Revenue has the right to immediately withdraw the deferral and collect the amount outstanding, along with a penalised interest rate of 8%.

Eligibility for a deferral is established by reference to the liability date in each year (1 November), i.e. the liable person must assess if he qualifies for a deferral at each liability date, as his personal circumstances may have changed since the liability date.

5.2 Income Threshold (Deferral Conditions Numbers 1–4)

The income threshold that determines whether a deferral may be claimed for a particular year is based on a person's gross income for the year. At the liability date each year, i.e. 1 May 2013 for 2013 and 1 November 2013 for 2014 (and each 1 November after that), a claimant must estimate what his likely gross income will be for that year. *Gross income* is all income before any deductions, allowances or reliefs that are allowed to be deducted when calculating a person's taxable income for income tax purposes. It includes income that is exempt from income tax and income received from the Department of Social Protection (DSP) but excludes Child Benefit payments.

The standard income thresholds may be increased where a claimant pays mortgage interest on their main or sole residence only (see below). The increase is limited to 80% of the gross interest (i.e. before tax relief at source is given) that is actually paid or that is likely to be paid in a particular year (*section 133*). As with gross income, a claimant must estimate at the liability date the amount of mortgage interest that is likely to be paid by the end of the year.

A property for which deferral is claimed must be the sole or main residence of the claimant and deferral based on income thresholds is not available for landlords or second homes.

Applications for deferral or partial deferral of LPT on the basis of income threshold may be made on the LPT return form by indicating the deferral condition number, from the following table, at Option 6 on the form. An LPT2 application form is not required for a deferral claimed under the income threshold criteria.

Income Threshold Criteria (*Section 132*)

	Deferral Condition Number	*Condition*
Full Deferral	1	Gross income for the year unlikely to exceed €15,000 (single or widow) and €25,000 (couple*).
Full Deferral	2	Gross income for the year unlikely to exceed the **adjusted income** limit. This adjusted income limit is calculated by **increasing** the €15,000 (single or widow) and €25,000 (couple*) thresholds by 80% of the expected gross mortgage interest payments.
Partial Deferral (50%)	3	Gross income for the year unlikely to exceed €25,000 (s/w) and €35,000 (couple*).
Partial Deferral (50%)	4	Gross income for the year unlikely to exceed the **adjusted income** limit. This adjusted income limit is calculated by increasing the €25,000 (single or widow) and €35,000 (couple*) thresholds by 80% of the expected gross mortgage interest payments.

* A *couple* includes a married couple, civil partners and certain cohabitants. Cohabitant is defined in section 172 of the Civil Partnership and Certain Rights and Obligations of Cohabitants Act 2010. For LPT deferral purposes, the required period of cohabitation is at least two years where the couple have children or at least five years where they do not have children.

EXAMPLE

Tessa Lisbon is a single owner-occupier of a residential property worth €230,000. Tessa earns €22,000 p.a. as of 1 May 2013 and has projected gross mortgage interest payments of €6,500 for 2013.

Her liability to LPT for 2013 is as follows:

Market Value	€230,000
Valuation band number	04
Valuation band	€200,000 to €250,000
Mid-point of valuation band	€225,000

LPT:	
€225,000 @ 0.18%	€405
LPT 2013 (50%)	€202
LPT 2014	€405

Tessa wishes to opt for a deferral of some or all of her LPT as she is struggling to live within her income.

Full Deferral:

Gross income threshold (single person)	€15,000
Plus: mortgage interest × 80% (€6,500 × 80%)	€5,200
Adjusted income threshold	€20,200

Full deferral is not available as Tessa's gross income €22,000 is greater than her adjusted income threshold €20,200.

Partial Deferral:

Gross income threshold (single person)	€25,000
Plus: mortgage interest × 80% (€6,500 × 80%)	€5,200
Adjusted income threshold	€30,200

Tessa is entitled to a partial deferral as her gross income €22,000 is less than her adjusted income threshold €30,200.

For 2013, Tessa must pay LPT of €101 and can defer €101.

If Tessa wishes to defer all or part of her 2014 liability, she must do the same calculation again for her income at 1 November 2013 (the liability date for 2014).

5.3 Personal Representative of a Deceased Liable Person (Deferral Condition Number 5)

Where a liable person who was the sole owner of a property dies, that person's personal representative may apply for a full deferral of LPT for a maximum period of three years commencing from the date of death (*section 133A*). Where the personal representative is in a position to transfer the property to a beneficiary of the estate or where it is sold within the three years, the deferral ends at that earlier time. A deferral can be claimed for:

- any LPT outstanding at the date of death,
- any LPT already deferred by the deceased person, and
- LPT becoming payable following death,

by submitting an LPT2 application form, along with the LPT1 return form.

5.4 Personal Insolvency (Deferral Condition Number 6)

A person who enters into any debt arrangement under the Personal Insolvency Act 2012 may apply for a deferral of LPT for the periods for which the insolvency arrangement is in place (*section 133B*). The deferred LPT plus interest will become due when the insolvency arrangement ceases. This deferral is open to all property owners, i.e. owner-occupiers and buy-to-let owners. The insolvency arrangement must be finalised between the liable person and the Insolvency Service of Ireland, and the case number quoted in the LPT2 application form.

5.5 Hardship (Deferral Condition Number 7)

Where a liable person suffers an unexpected and unavoidable significant financial loss or expense within the current year, and is unable to pay the LPT without causing excessive financial hardship, then that person can apply for a full or partial deferral (*section 133C*). Claims for this type of deferral will require full disclosure, on the LPT2 application form, of the particular loss or expense, details of the person's financial circumstances and any other information required by Revenue.

Following an examination of the information provided, Revenue will determine whether to grant a deferral (full or partial) but will not refund any payments made by the liable person up to that point.

Losses or expenses that will be considered in hardship claims are:

- emergency and/or significant medical expenses;
- expenses incurred as a result of a serious accident or death of a family member;
- significant and unexpected repairs to a private home necessary to return/maintain the house to/in a habitable condition;
- loss of employment; and/or
- a significant bad debt or trading loss incurred by a self-employed person.

Any mitigation of such a loss through, say, an insurance claim or a redundancy payment received, etc., will be taken into account by Revenue when determining the claim.

In order to be considered for a deferral, the loss suffered by the liable person must reduce the remainder of his income to the income threshold levels at **Section 5.2** above, or, the total loss suffered must be at least 20% of his gross income. However, it does not follow that if either or both of these conditions are met, deferral will be granted automatically. The onus is on the liable person to demonstrate that payment of the tax would cause excessive financial hardship.

In considering the question of hardship, the liable person's personal circumstances may be taken into account. For example, whether the house is occupied by other household members who, although not liable for LPT, may have income and would be expected to contribute to household payments.

EXAMPLE

Brian and Joan are a married couple who own their own home and a second rental property (which they own outright) that is currently unoccupied. They estimate they will make mortgage interest payments on their private residence of €16,000 in 2013. Their estimated gross income for 2013 is €55,000. The rental property suffered severe storm damage, requiring repairs costing €20,000 and for which Brian and Joan were not insured.

Adjusted Gross Income:

Gross income	€55,000
Less: unexpected significant expense	€(20,000)
Adjusted gross income	€35,000

Adjusted Income Threshold:	**Full Deferral**	**Partial Deferral**
Gross income threshold (couple)	€25,000	€35,000
Plus: mortgage interest × 80% (€16,000 × 80%)	€12,800	€12,800
Adjusted income threshold	€37,800	€47,800

As the unexpected significant expense is both greater than 20% of their gross income and reduces the adjusted gross income below the income threshold for a full deferral, Revenue may consider an application for a full deferral. Appropriate documentary evidence must be provided in support of the claim that, as a result of the repairs bill, payment of the tax would cause excessive hardship.

EXAMPLE

Julie, who is single, has an estimated gross income of €50,000 for 2013. She estimates that her mortgage interest will be €10,000 in 2013. Julie's mother Mary had a serious accident in a holiday resort abroad, and Julie incurred significant expenses of €25,000 to travel abroad and to pay her mother's medical bills. Mary was not insured but Julie did manage to secure a small amount of compensation of €5,000 from the resort owner.

Adjusted Gross Income:

Gross Income	€50,000
Less: Unexpected significant expense	€(25,000)
Plus: Compensation received	€ 5,000
Adjusted gross income	€30,000

Adjusted Income Threshold:	Full Deferral	Partial Deferral
Gross Income Threshold (single)	€15,000	€25,000
Plus: mortgage interest × 80% (€10,000 × 80%)	€8,000	€8,000
Adjusted Income Threshold	€23,000	€33,000

As the unexpected significant expense is greater than 20% of Julie's gross income, Revenue may consider an application for a full deferral. However, if granted, this will only be a partial deferral as her adjusted gross income is above the threshold amount for a full deferral but is below the threshold amount for a partial deferral. Again, appropriate documentary evidence must be provided in support of the claim that, as a result of the accident, payment of the tax would cause excessive hardship.

5.6 Refusal of a Deferral

If Revenue refuse to grant a full or partial deferral, Revenue must notify the liable person in writing. The liable person then has 14 days to appeal the Revenue decision by giving a written Notice of Appeal, stating the grounds of his appeal. The liable person must also self-assess and pay the LPT due pending the outcome of his appeal, which will be determined by the Appeal Commissioners in the same way as any appeal against a Revenue assessment (*section 135*).

5.7 Cessation of a Deferral

A deferred amount on a relevant property becomes payable when the property is sold or if the liable person is in receipt of a windfall gain (*section 139*). It is not clear, however, how much the windfall gain must be in order for the deferred amount to 'crystallise', but one would assume that the gain should be of such significance to comfortably pay off any outstanding amount of deferred LPT and interest. Where a property is transferred by way of gift or inheritance, the deferral remains in place until the next liability date (1 November each year), after which Revenue may allow the deferral to continue if the new liable person applies for and satisfies, in their own right, the conditions for deferral.

If a liable person ceases to meet the income thresholds due to a change in circumstances, any deferral allowed before the change is allowed to continue, but the deferral of any LPT from the date of the change in circumstances will cease. The liable person is obliged to inform Revenue immediately of any change that no longer entitles that person to the deferral. Where a spouse, civil partner or cohabitant dies and the couple, prior to the death, claimed deferral on income threshold grounds, the liable person may still continue to claim the deferral until the next valuation date, irrespective of whether or not the surviving liable person no longer satisfies the deferral thresholds.

EXAMPLE

John Mills and his wife Christine had an annual joint income of €24,000 and qualified for and claimed a full deferral of LPT on income grounds. Christine passed away in October 2013 and John's income was reduced to €18,000 per annum. While John's income, for a full deferral of LPT, exceeds the annual threshold limit of €15,000 for a single person, John can continue to claim a full deferral on income grounds until 1 November 2016 (the next valuation date). If John's circumstances remain unchanged at that date he may claim for a partial deferral of LPT for the years 2017 *et seq.* and the full deferral up until 1 November 2016 remains in place.

5.8 Payments on Account

A liable person who has been allowed a deferral can make a full or partial payment against the deferred amount at any time. Any amounts paid are credited against earlier amounts of LPT due in priority to more recent liabilities. A payment on account against LPT deferred does not terminate a deferral arrangement if the liable person's circumstances are such that they still qualify for a full or partial deferral. The deferred amount remains a charge on the property and cannot exceed the chargeable value of the property at the last liability date.

6

Local Property Tax and Other Taxes

6.1 Introduction

As discussed in **Chapter 1**, the obligation to pay local property tax (LPT) is conferred upon a liable person by virtue of the Finance (Local Property Tax) Act 2012, as amended ('the Act'). A designated liable person is the owner who, where property is in joint ownership, is designated with the task of filing the LPT return and making the payment. Where that person is also a "chargeable person" within the meaning of section 957A of the Taxes Consolidation Act 1997 (TCA 1997) the obligation to file and pay LPT becomes very significant.

6.2 Surcharge for Late Filing by a "Chargeable Person"

A *chargeable person* (which includes a company) is one who is obliged to file an income tax, corporation tax or capital gains tax (IT/CT/CGT) return each year. While most chargeable persons are companies, self-employed taxpayers and proprietary directors, many PAYE employees are also chargeable persons where they have significant non-PAYE income even if the employee has no taxable non-PAYE income. An example would be a PAYE employee who has rental properties and substantial rental income, but has no tax liability on that income because of large interest and running costs deductible against the rental income.

Under the TCA 1997, a chargeable person is liable to a tax surcharge where an IT/CT/CGT return is not filed by the specified return date. Under the Act, a chargeable person, who is also a designated liable person for LPT purposes, is liable to a tax surcharge on their IT/CT/CGT tax liability if they do not file and pay an LPT return.

In other words, if a chargeable person fails to file an LPT return before the IT/CT/CGT return is filed he or she is liable to a tax surcharge of 10% of the amount of the IT/CT/CGT liability (irrespective of how much is actually due).

EXAMPLE

John is a self-employed carpenter and a chargeable person for income tax. John owns a residential property and, based on its chargeable value, owes LPT of €203 for 2013. John files his 2012 income tax return in October 2013, which shows a gross tax liability of €12,000 less preliminary tax paid of €9,000. Because John has not filed his LPT return a surcharge of 10% of €12,000 is applied to his IT liability for the non-filing and payment of the 2013 LPT return (due on 7 May 2013).

Where the LPT return is filed subsequent to the filing of an IT/CT/CGT return the surcharge is reduced to the actual amount of the LPT due, which is payable in addition to the LPT amount plus any interest due.

EXAMPLE

John (from the above example) has suffered a surcharge of €1,200 for the non-filing and payment of his LPT return and decides to file his LPT return in December 2013. The LPT surcharge is reduced to €203 and John is also liable for the LPT due of €203 plus any interest arising for the late payment.

Only one surcharge is applied if a chargeable person fails to file or is late in filing an IT/CT/CGT return and an LPT return. It should be noted that the late filing surcharges for IT/CT/CGT differ slightly from the LPT surcharges in that a 5% surcharge applies to an IT/CT/CGT return submitted within two months of the specified return date and a 10% surcharge applies to any return submitted after two months.

EXAMPLE

> John (from the above example) does not file his 2012 income tax return until December 2013 and at that time his LPT return for 2013 is still outstanding. As he is late filing his IT return, John will suffer an income tax late filing surcharge of 5% of the gross income tax due, i.e. €600. He is not liable to any further surcharge for the non-filing of his LPT return.

It should be stressed that the late filing and payment of an LPT return does not in itself generate a surcharge but only if the LPT return is filed **after** the date the IT/CT/CGT return is filed. Where an LPT return is filed late but before the date of filing the IT/CT/CGT return, a surcharge does not arise. If the IT/CT/CGT return is filed early, it is on this date (and not the due date of the return) that the LPT surcharge is imposed provided, of course, that it occurs after the LPT due date.

6.3 The Household Charge and Local Property Tax

The Household Charge was introduced for 2012 only by the Local Government (Household Charge) Act 2011 and was a flat charge of €100 per qualifying residential property, ultimately payable to the local authorities.

Any Household Charge that remains unpaid as of 1 July 2013 is increased to €200 and becomes part of any LPT due for 2013. It will only be collected by the Revenue Commissioners and will be subject to the same surcharge and interest rules as LPT (see **Section 6.2**).

EXAMPLE

Joan is a chargeable person and a designated liable person for LPT for the property which she shares with her partner Denise. Joan did not pay the Household Charge from 2012, but has filed and paid her LPT return on time.

Joan files her 2012 income tax return in October 2013 with a gross tax liability of €10,000. Even though Joan has filed and paid her LPT and income tax returns on time, the Household Charge arrears are treated as outstanding LPT and an LPT surcharge of 10%, i.e. €1,000 arises.

Once Joan pays the outstanding Household Charge amount of €200, the LPT surcharge is capped at €200.

6.4 Local Property Tax and Relationship with Other Taxes

One of the strongest tax collection tools that the Revenue Commissioners have is the ability, under the TCA 1997, to offset any amounts of tax, interest and penalties due against any tax refunds owed to a person or a company. Section 120 of the Act confers on Revenue the same powers of collection for LPT as they have for all the other taxes.

7

Procedures and Enforcement

7.1 Introduction

The Revenue Commissioners issued nearly 1.67 million local property tax letters to people in early 2013. In many cases the letter included a "Notice of Estimate of Local Property Tax Payable" and a "Return for Local Property Tax" form (LPT1). For others, the letter merely stated that the taxpayer had a liability to LPT and to file online using the Revenue On-line Service (ROS). While the vast majority of those contacted (93% as of Revenue's data at February 2014) are deemed to have complied with the filing requirements and payment of LPT, the remaining 10% are now firmly in Revenue's sights for further investigation.

7.2 Compliant Taxpayers

In summary, those who are deemed compliant for LPT purposes are those who:

- made an LPT return and paid or set out a payment arrangement for the LPT due;
- contacted Revenue to inform them that they are not the liable person for that property;
- made an LPT return and claimed an exemption as allowed under the Act (see **Chapter 2**);
- made an LPT return and claimed a deferral or partial deferral of the LPT due (see **Chapter 5**).

Compliant taxpayers need do no more for the tax year 2014 except to confirm a payment method for the 2014 tax where the 2013 payment was not made under a phased payment arrangement (e.g. direct debit or deduction at source from salary, pension, Department of Social Protection (DSP) payment, etc.). For those who chose any other payment method (e.g. single debit instruction/cash or cheque payment) they must have confirmed the payment method for 2014 by:

- 7 November 2013, if confirmed by paper, or
- 27 November 2013, if confirmed online.

7.3 Non-compliant Taxpayers

Those who either did not contact Revenue or did not make an LPT return will be pursued by Revenue, who will attempt to collect the Revenue's estimate of LPT which accompanied the original LPT letters. Where the liable person does make a return but fails to honour the method of payment specified, Revenue may also seek to have the amounts due collected using the following collection options:

- mandatory deduction of the Revenue estimate of LPT or LPT due but unpaid from salaries, pensions, DSP payments and Department of Agriculture, Food and the Marine (DAFM) payments (*sections 66, 85* and *103*);
- withholding of any other tax refund due as payment against the LPT due;
- attachment of the LPT amount owed against bank accounts where Revenue secures an order to force a bank to deduct the LPT amount from the taxpayer's bank account and pay over the liability to Revenue;
- referral of debt to a Sheriff for collection.

In addition to the collection of the tax due, Revenue may impose other sanctions and penalties including:

- an LPT surcharge of 10% of overall IT/CT/CGT tax liability for chargeable persons (see **Chapter 6**);
- a penalty for non-filing of an LPT return equal to the amount of LPT due, subject to a maximum penalty of €3,000;
- interest payable of 0.0219% per day or part thereof (approximately 8% per annum) (payable from the due date – see **Section 4.2**);
- non-issue of a tax clearance certificate;

- where LPT remains outstanding, a charge will attach to the property. This charge will have to be discharged on the sale/ transfer of the property.

7.3.1 Mandatory Deduction of the Revenue Estimate of LPT from Salaries, Pensions and Government Payments

Before enforcing a mandatory deduction for LPT, Revenue will issue a reminder letter to the liable person who has not as yet filed a return and/or paid LPT. The letter will state that Revenue will issue an instruction to the person's named employer/pension provider/relevant government department to deduct the amount of the Revenue estimate for LPT, or the LPT amount unpaid, in equal instalments from a stated date. The liable person then has seven days to either file a return online or contact Revenue if he or she is not the liable person.

Once Revenue has issued a deduction notice to the employer/ pension provider, etc. (e.g. a revised P2C) showing the amount of LPT to be deducted, the liable person must engage directly with Revenue if he or she wishes for the deduction to cease or to be amended. Employers/pension providers will not know from the P2C (employer tax credit certificate) whether the LPT was chosen voluntarily or imposed mandatorily.

Note: a mandatory deduction does not absolve the need for a liable person to make an LPT return; indeed, the penalty for non-filing still applies. If the Revenue estimate is collected through deduction at source, interest will not also be deducted. Any general imposition of interest will be notified by Revenue in advance.

7.3.2 Self-assessed Taxpayers

In many respects the penalties for the non-filing and paying of LPT are much more onerous for self-assessed taxpayers. Revenue will not issue a tax clearance certificate where LPT is due and an LPT surcharge based on the chargeable persons income tax, corporation tax or CGT liability can be imposed for the late or non-filing of the LPT return, regardless of whether or not the IT/CT/CGT return is submitted on time (see **Chapter 6**). Note, however, that in order for these penalties to be applied to the self-assessed person, he or she must be both:

- a chargeable person (i.e. liable to self-assessment under IT/CT/CGT rules); AND
- the designated liable person for LPT.

EXAMPLE

Bill Potts and Mary Walsh, a married couple, are joint owners of their family home and a holiday home in Wexford. Bill is a self-employed dentist and Mary works as a biochemist for the local hospital and is a PAYE employee. Mary paid the Household Charge in 2012 for both properties and, as a consequence, received the Revenue letter and return in respect of the LPT. She is therefore deemed to be the designated liable person. Bill files and pays his income tax return on time in October 2013, but Mary fails to pay and file the LPT return. As Bill is not the designated liable person for LPT, he is not subject to the LPT surcharge on his 2012 income tax return. As Mary has a PAYE source of income, Revenue will seek to enforce a mandatory deduction from her wages of the Revenue estimate amount of LPT for the two properties.

7.4 Revenue Inquiries

While Revenue will not challenge an assessment where a liable person makes a self-assessment based on the Revenue valuation guidelines (on properties under €1 million in value) and pays the amount of the LPT self-assessment (*section 15*), Revenue are entitled to make any inquiry (within four years of the relevant liability date) where:

- Revenue has reason to believe that the LPT return does not contain a full and true disclosure of all material facts necessary for the establishment of the local property tax payable by the liable person in relation to a liability date; or

- Revenue has reason to believe that the liable person has engaged in deliberate or careless behaviour in connection with local property tax payable in relation to a liability date; or

- the liable person fails to deliver a return in relation to a particular liability date (*section 141*).

This inquiry is an important Revenue power as it effectively gives Revenue the right to review any LPT return if they have any suspicions as to its veracity.

Under this right of inquiry, Revenue can query whether:

- the property is a relevant residential property on a liability date (see **Sections 2.2** and **2.3**);
- the person is a liable person on a liability date;
- the chargeable value of a relevant residential property on a valuation date is accurate (see **Section 2.4**);
- the liable person is eligible for a deferral as claimed;
- the liable person is entitled to an exemption as claimed;
- any return, statement or particulars prepared and delivered under the Act are accurate.

7.4.1 *Inquiry as to whether a Property is a Relevant Residential Property on a Liability Date*

A Revenue inquiry may arise where a person states that a property is not a relevant residential property and does not give an adequate reason for this declaration.

EXAMPLE

The old farm house on James's farm fell into disrepair after his father passed away 15 years ago. James uses the old farmhouse as a shelter for cattle and has maintained the ESB supply to the house since his father's death in order to pump water and run an electric fence. James received an LPT return for the property and contacted Revenue to say that the farmhouse was unoccupied and not a residential property. Revenue checked with the ESB records and established that there had been a consistent electricity supply to the property for over 25 years. Revenue contacted James requiring more proof and explanation as to why the property was declared as not being a residential property. James provided photographic evidence of the state of the property and a more detailed explanation of its use. On the basis of this inquiry, Revenue was satisfied that the property was not a residential property at the liability date.

7.4.2 Inquiry as to whether the Person is a Liable Person on a Liability Date

In most instances it would appear that this Revenue inquiry may arise where a person has stated that they are not the liable person and where they either cannot or will not identify the liable person.

For example, while a tenant may be unsure as to who the owner is, the rent on the property is payable to a person who may or may not be the liable person but who can probably provide Revenue with further information as to the identity of the liable person. In addition to the power of inquiry under *section 141*, Revenue also has the authority under *section 46* of the Act to require any lessee or occupant of a property to provide information in relation to a lessor/landlord where it has reasonable grounds for believing that the occupant is likely to have relevant information in relation to the liable person.

Failure or refusal to comply with a notice requesting information issued by Revenue may leave an occupant liable to a penalty of €1,000.

7.4.3 Inquiry as to whether the Chargeable Value of a Relevant Residential Property on a Valuation Date is Accurate

It appears that the most likely trigger of a Revenue inquiry under this heading would be a substantially different valuation of a property from the neighbourhood 'norm'. For example, if all the houses in the "Woodvale" estate are four-bed, detached homes and the majority of the LPT returns put the value of the properties in valuation band 5 or 6 (i.e. between €250,000 and €350,000), a declared chargeable value, of the same type of property, at valuation band number 1 (< €100,000) will probably trigger a Revenue inquiry.

Where a property is valued at greater than €1 million, Revenue may request some further information verifying the value of the property (e.g. an auctioneer's valuation, sale contracts if the house changed hands in the recent past, etc.) as the Revenue guidelines with regard to inquiries do not apply to properties valued at greater than €1 million.

7.4.4 Inquiry as to whether the Liable Person is Eligible for a Deferral as Claimed

Revenue may make inquiries where it comes to their attention that the circumstances resulting in a claim for deferral have changed or where the claim for deferral was made dishonestly. Revenue may also make additional inquiries for supporting documentation where a liable person claims a deferral on hardship grounds. It is a condition of any claim for a deferral that, if the liable person's circumstances change and this affects the basis on which the deferral was claimed, the liable person must contact Revenue, as the liable person may no longer meet the conditions for qualifying for the deferral.

EXAMPLE

Cory Amos owns a residential property and was unemployed at the valuation date of 1 May 2013. He estimated that his adjusted income for LPT deferral on income grounds (see **Section 5.2**) for 2013 would be €14,200, as adjusted by 80% of his mortgage interest payable of €5,000.

Cory returned his LPT return on time claiming a deferral from LPT under deferral condition number 1 (income threshold) (see **Chapter 5**). On 28 October 2013, Cory was offered a job paying €30,000 per annum, commencing in January 2014. As he will no longer qualify for a deferral on income grounds in 2014, he must contact Revenue and make arrangements for the payment of the 2014 LPT. If the new job was paying €18,000 Cory could continue to claim a deferral as, while his circumstances have changed, he is still entitled to a deferral under condition number 2 (adjusted income threshold) as his adjusted income threshold of €19,000 (€15,000 + (80% × €5,000)) is still greater than his income.

7.4.5 *Inquiry as to whether the Liable Person is Entitled to an Exemption as Claimed*

This is possibly the category where the most inquiries may be made as, while a deferral merely defers the payment of LPT and interest to a later date, an exemption absolves the liable person from paying any LPT.

A property may cease to be exempt, for example, where an exemption was claimed under Exemption Type A (new, completed and unoccupied property purchased from a builder) the exemption ceases if the property is sold.

Revenue will check that exemptions claimed for properties in so called "ghost estates" are for properties in estates listed in the Finance (Local Property Tax) Regulations (S.I. No. 91 of 2013) and where an exemption is claimed for pyritic damage, a certificate under the Finance (Local Property Tax) (Pyrite Exemption) Regulations 2013 (S.I. No. 147 of 2103) has been issued.

Again, it is also the case that if the basis for the exemption ceases the liable person must contact Revenue and inform them of the change in circumstances (e.g. where a commercial guest house previously paying commercial rates ceases to trade and reverts to being a private residential property, the property becomes liable to LPT).

7.5 Appeals

Where there is a disagreement between an individual and Revenue on matters relating to LPT (such as whether the property is residential, who the liable person is, disputed valuations, denial of deferrals/exemptions, etc.) which cannot be resolved, Revenue will issue a formal notice of assessment or a formal decision or determination. The individual may appeal to the Appeal Commissioners against those notices and request a determination.

As with other self-assessed taxes, in order to appeal Revenue's assessment, the individual must have made an LPT return and paid his or her assessment of the tax due (even if this is disputed).

8

Section-by-section Analysis of the Local Property Tax Legislation[1]

Part 1 – Preliminary and General

Section 2 – Interpretation

This is the definition section for the Act. Many of the definitions are technical in nature, but a few are of direct interest and relevance. These include:

"Building"
The term "building" includes part of a building, and a structure of any kind, provided that structure is permanently attached to the ground. Houseboats and mobile homes are excluded.

"Chargeable Value"
This means the price the residential property might reasonably be expected to fetch from a sale in the open market. The definition refers to the unencumbered value of the property, i.e. before taking into account any debt on the property, typically a mortgage. The deal has to be done in such a way as to ensure that the vendor received the best price for the property. The chargeable value is based on a valuation of the property that ignores any issues related to access, as the property is deemed to enjoy the same ease of access as was enjoyed before the sale.

---

[1] Finance (Local Property Tax) Act 2012 (as amended up to and including Finance (Local Property Tax) (Amendment) Act 2013).

"Liability Date"
Generally, the liability date for LPT will be 1 November in the year preceding the tax year. In other words, for the tax year 2014, the liability date will be 1 November 2013.

"Residential Property"
Under the Act, "'residential property' means any building or structure which is in use as, or is suitable for use as, a dwelling and includes any shed, outhouse, garage or other building or structure and any yard, garden or other land" connected with the building.

This is one of the most important definitions in the Act. Tax will not be payable on any property that is not suitable for use as a dwelling. However, a residential property will include sheds, outhouses, garages, if they exist. A "residential property" also includes any yard or garden or other plot of ground associated with the house. However, the total land to be associated with a residential property is not to exceed one acre. This definition ties in with the earlier definition of "chargeable value". Taken together, the amount on which the liable person pays tax is the total of the value of the house, the outbuildings, yards and gardens, up to a maximum of one acre.

Part 2 – Residential Property

Section 3 – Meaning of Relevant Residential Property

Though this section seems to state the obvious, it is significant. A residential property only becomes a "relevant" residential property if it is a residential property on the liability date, i.e. the date on which one decides whether a property is within the charge to tax, usually 1 November in the year preceding the tax year. If the property is not suitable for use as a dwelling, and was not used as a dwelling on the liability date, the tax charge does not arise.

Section 4 – Residential Property Fully Subject to Municipal Rates

This exemption excludes any residential properties that are subject to local authority rates from the charge to tax.

Section 5 – Long-term Mental or Physical Infirmity

An exemption applies to property that is vacant for at least 12 months, where the householder has been ill or infirm. If the property has not been vacant a full 12 months, but a suitably qualified doctor is satisfied that the householder is unlikely ever to be able to return and live there again on their own, the property will also be excluded from the charge to tax. The intention is to provide relief for people who are living in nursing homes and have left their houses vacant. A further measure in section 5 ensures that nursing homes are exempt from the LPT.

Section 6 – Newly Constructed Residential Properties

Section 6 covers situations in which houses are newly constructed. There are four tests, **each** of which must be met, if the LPT is not to apply:

1. the house is completed, but not yet sold by the builder or developer;
2. it must not be occupied as a dwelling;
3. it must not have generated any taxable income for its owner; and
4. it must be treated in the accounts of the builder or developer as part of the stock in trade.

Section 7 – Special Needs Accommodation

This section relates to properties that are provided as special needs accommodation. "Special needs" has a particular meaning: accommodation provided to persons who by reason of old age, physical or mental disability or other cause require special accommodation and support to enable them to live in their community. Such properties have to be owned either by a charity or by a body established by statute (e.g. a public body such as the HSE).

Section 7A – Properties used by a Charity for Recreational Activities

This new section was inserted by the Finance (Local Property Tax) (Amendment) Bill 2013. Its purpose is to provide an exemption for residential properties where the liable person is a charity, and where the premises are used for recreational purposes. The intention is to exempt properties used by voluntary organisations for summer camps, and so forth.

Section 8 – Exemption for First-time Buyers

Section 8 was written to provide an exemption for first-time buyers and was tied to the definition of first-time buyer for the purposes of mortgage interest relief in section 244 of the Taxes Consolidation Act 1997 (TCA 1997). However, due to a drafting error, the section is deemed to apply to **any** purchaser who:

- purchased the property in the calendar year **2013 only**; *and*
- occupied the property as a sole or main residence since the purchase in 2013.

The exemption is a limited exemption and applies in respect of the liability dates in the years 2013, 2014 and 2015. There were two liability dates in 2013: 1 May and 1 November. Accordingly, the exemption applies for 3.5 years:

- the half-year payment of 2013 (liability date 1 May 2013);
- the full-year payment for 2014 (liability date 1 November 2013);
- the full-year payment for 2015 (liability date 1 November 2014); *and*
- the full-year payment for 2016 (liability date 1 November 2015).

The exemption will cease to apply if the property on which the exemption is being claimed is sold or ceases to be used as the sole or main residence of the purchaser at any time after the purchase of the property.

Section 9 – Purchase of New Residential Properties in the Period 2013 to 2016

Section 9 concerns new residential properties bought in the period from 2013 to 2016. It is tied in with section 6, described above, which exempts newly constructed properties. If the newly constructed properly would have been exempt under section 6, and is sold for the **first time** at any time between 1 January 2013 and 31 October 2016, it will not be regarded as a taxable property in respect of any liability dates between the first time it is purchased and 31 October 2016.

In effect, this is another 3.5-year exemption. Four liability dates fall into the period covered by section 9, and exempt:

- the half-year payment for 2013 (liability date 1 May 2013);
- the full-year payment for 2014 (liability date 1 November 2013);

- the full-year payment for 2015 (liability date 1 November 2014); and
- the full-year payment for 2016 (liability date 1 November 2015).

The exemption expires the day before the liability date for 2017.

> *Note*: this exemption only applies on a property and its first owners. If the property is sold within the exemption period, the second buyers cannot avail of the benefit of the exemption.

Section 10 – Unfinished Housing Estates

This section 10 deals with unfinished or "ghost estates". It simply states that a residential property that is situated in an unfinished housing estate shall not be regarded as a relevant residential property and, accordingly, not be liable to LPT.

The bulk of section 10 deals with a procedure whereby the Minister for the Environment, Community and Local Government can identify unfinished estates and what he has to take into account when identifying an unfinished estate. The key point here is that the householder cannot themselves decide whether or not they are living in an unfinished or ghost estate – the estate must receive certification from the Minister for the Environment, Community and Local Government and be included on the list of unfinished estates as prescribed by the said Minister.

Section 10A – Pyrite-induced Damage

The Minister for the Environment, Community and Local Government is given power in this section to certify properties that suffer from pyrite-induced damage and thereby temporarily exempt them from LPT. Some residential developments, mainly in north Leinster, were constructed using a form of building aggregate containing minerals known as pyrite. Unfortunately, these aggregates can react badly to damp conditions and swell, thereby causing structural damage.

Where a residential property is certified by the Minister for the Environment, Community and Local Government as described, it will be exempt from LPT for the liability date after which the certificate is received, and the following two liability dates.

The year 2013 is anomalous in that, as noted above, there are two liability dates:

- 1 May 2013; and
- 1 November 2013.

If the householder receives the certificate of pyrite exemption before the end of 2013, he or she may elect to have either 1 May 2013 or 1 November 2013 treated as the first of the three liability dates for the purposes of this temporary exemption. All things being equal, householders in this situation should probably opt for 1 November 2013 because the LPT collected by reference to 1 May 2013 is for a half-year, not a full year.

Section 10B – Permanently and Totally Incapacitated Individuals

Another more recent addition to the legislation was a special exemption for residential properties occupied by permanently and totally incapacitated individuals. However, the exemption ceases to apply where the residential property is sold, unless the individual continues to live in the property, which is his or her sole main residence.

Part 3 – Liable Person

Part 3 of the Act moves away from considering what kind of properties are liable to *who* is liable.

Section 11 – Liable Persons

Section 11 is possibly one of the most important sections in the Act.

In tax law, a 'person' also includes a company, a partnership or a trust. It does not just mean a natural person or individual. Accordingly, this section is equally as relevant to companies as it is to individuals.

The basic rule is that if you own any property outright, or have an entitlement to a property for a period of 20 years or more, you become liable for the LPT on that property. Similarly, if you are the landlord and have an entitlement to rents and profits from that property for a period of 20 years or more, you are the liable person.

Thus, you do not actually have to be *resident* in the property to be liable; nor must you own it outright. You might have a 99-year lease, or other form of long lease, on the property, perhaps subject to ground rent.

Section 11 acknowledges that co-ownership frequently arises. If every person involved in a property holds an equal share, then all persons become liable in relation to the property. This is typically the situation with married couples – both spouses are equally liable. This does not mean that LPT has to be paid twice, but it allows Revenue to pursue either one or the other spouse in relation to the liability for the whole property.

Where the property is in multiple ownership, multiple persons can equally be liable. The only exception is where one or more of the co-owners have an interest in the property of less than 20 years' duration. This might occur, for example, where a part of a property is sublet on a shorter lease to another person.

The main rule to bear in mind is that if a person holds any form of ownership over a residential property for a period of 20 or more years, they become liable for LPT, irrespective of who else might be involved in the ownership.

Ownership is defined quite widely. It is possible, for example, to have a right or entitlement to a residential property without a formal legal ownership. This type of ownership is often referred to as a *beneficial interest*. If that beneficial interest gives you a right to possess the property for 20 years or more, or draw rents from the property for 20 years or more, you become liable to LPT. A similar rule applies if you are the trustee or the beneficiary of an estate including a residential property.

If you are a life tenant, or have a right of occupation to a property for a period that may be 20 years or more, you become liable. Being a *life tenant* means having an entitlement to live in the property for the period of your own life, or for the period of someone else's life. Such situations arise typically as a result of a gift or inheritance. However, you will only be liable if you have an exclusive right of residence, not shared with anyone else. *Note:* this condition is triggered by right of residence – you must actually live in the property to become liable under this section.

Another slightly unusual aspect is that the personal representative of a deceased person's estate becomes liable for any LPT on residential properties within the estate. Normally, when a person dies, any outstanding taxes become a liability of his or her estate. Once those taxes have been paid out of the estate, the balance can be distributed appropriately to the beneficiaries, usually in accordance with the deceased person's will. For LPT the situation is slightly different. It is the personal representative, rather than the estate, which must meet the liability. There is provision under the Succession Act 1955 for the personal representative to reclaim the money from the estate as an expense of administration.

Section 11 provides for two situations where otherwise a residential property might slip through the cracks for the collection of the tax.

One technical provision ensures that if you are in possession of a residential property, but your title has yet to be registered with the Land Registry Office, you remain as the liable person. This is to deal with situations where the passage of title has not been formally completed on a purchase or inheritance. Another, added by the Finance (Local Property Tax) (Amendment) Act 2013, ensures that in situations where a householder dies intestate (i.e. without leaving a will) and there is no executor or personal representative appointed, the person occupying the property, or receiving rents from the property, becomes the liable person for LPT.

Section 12 – Occupation or Receipt of Rents or Profits as Evidence of Liability

As we have seen above, section 11 deals with slightly unusual cases where title to property is not straightforward or is in transition. Section 12 effectively leaves the onus, in the case of any dispute, on the taxpayer to establish who is properly liable. The presumption will always be that the person who is occupying the property, or who is the landlord of the property, will be the liable person. Section 12 also ensures that Revenue can raise estimates or assessments or request returns, etc., without first inquiring as to the title attached to the property.

Part 4 – Charging Provisions

Section 13 – Valuation Date

This section introduces the concept of a *valuation date*. This is not to be confused with the *liability date*. The liability date is the anchor against which the ownership of the property, or any exemption, etc., is determined. The valuation date, on the other hand, is the date on which the value is set.

The main reason there is a difference between the valuation date and the liability date is that for the first four years of operation of LPT, i.e. 2013, 2014, 2015 and 2016, the valuation date will always be 1 May 2013. In this way, the legislation allows the valuation established for the first payment of tax to persist for the next three payments as well. The liable person might change, or the status of the property might change by reference to the liability date, but irrespective of any of those changes, the valuation to be used is that which applied on 1 May 2013.

The notion of the value remaining valid for a three-year period also applies after 2016. For the payment dates in 2017, 2018 and 2019, the valuation date will be 1 November 2016. For the payment dates in 2020, 2021 and 2022, the valuation date will be 1 November 2019, and so on.

Section 14 – Change of Liable Person between Consecutive Valuation Dates

Section 14 provides that the valuation will not change between one valuation date and the next valuation date, even if the liable person changes. However, where there is a change of liable person (typically as a result of a change of ownership) the person who is selling the property must pass on the details of the current valuation for LPT purposes. This might involve simply telling the new liable person what valuation was used in the last return, or providing a copy of the return, or providing any Revenue estimate which issued because a return had not been submitted.

Section 14 also states that if a property is not a relevant residential property on 1 May 2013 then no LPT is due for three years, even if there is a change of ownership.

Section 15 – Valuation in Accordance with Revenue Guidelines

This section requires Revenue to provide guidelines to household-ers as to how to come up with a valuation for LPT. As long as the householder makes a self-assessment of the value of the property following these Revenue guidelines, and then pays the tax based on that self-assessment, Revenue will not challenge the amount. This is an important protection in law – it would be a good defence, if challenged, to show that the Revenue guidelines were followed in good faith in arriving at the property value, upon which the LPT was paid. However, this protection won't apply if the value of the property is in excess of €1 million.

Section 15A – Property Adapted for Use by Disabled Persons

This section provides some relief for property that has been adapted for use by disabled persons. Where a house has been adapted, and received grant aid for the adaptation, the chargeable value of the house for LPT purposes is reduced by the lesser of the value of the work carried out or the maximum grant payable. The person with the disability has to occupy the property as his or her sole or main residence. The discounted value will continue to apply – it is not just a once-off relief for the year in which the adaptation was made. If further adaptations are carried out, they will also serve to further reduce the chargeable value.

The grants that are taken into account are those paid under the Housing (Adaptation Grants for Older People and People with a Disability) Regulations 2007 (S.I. No. 670 of 2007), or under regu-lation 4 of the Housing (Disabled Persons and Essential Repairs Grants) Regulations 2001 (S.I. No. 607 of 2001). *Note,* however, that the calculation of the relief is not contingent on the actual grant amounts paid but on the maximum grant payable under these regu-lations, having reference to the age of the property.

Section 16 – Charge to Local Property Tax

Section 16 is something of a formality. Every piece of tax legislation has to explicitly state that a tax is going to be charged, even where the entire point of the legislation is to specify who, what, when and by which amount. Section 16 is that statement that tax will be charged.

The section does, however, contain another important protection, to the effect that LPT may be paid by another person on behalf of the person who was properly liable. The intention here is, for example, that a son could pay his father's LPT. This provision might seem trivial until we consider the interaction of other elements of the tax code. The payment of LPT by one individual on behalf of another will not be treated, for example, as a gift or a payment of income for the purposes of the other taxes. Family members, therefore, can help each other with LPT payments without any concerns regarding implications for inheritance taxes, etc.

Section 17 – Amount of Local Property Tax

Section 17 contains a table with which to calculate the amount of LPT due. There are two steps to the valuation process. The first is to come up with a value. Most will do that in accordance with the Revenue guidelines, which are described in section 15. Secondly, the valuation will then fall into a band and the tax to be paid is linked to that band.

For the first four years of the existence of the LPT, the tax rate applicable to each band is 0.18%. The amount to be paid is 0.18% of the midpoint of the band. For example, if the valuation is €260,000, that valuation falls into the band €250,001–€300,000 and the tax payable is calculated as being 0.18% of €275,000, or €495. Equally, however, a valuation of €290,000 falls into the same band. Therefore the tax payable is the same: €495.

The table of bands only goes as far as €1 million. If the valuation exceeds €1 million, the first €1 million is charged at 0.18%, or €1,800. Any amount in excess of €1 million is charged at 0.25%, without the valuation band system being applied. For example, if a property is valued at €2 million, the LPT will be €1,800 (€1 million × 0.18%) + €2,500 (€1 million × 0.25%), i.e. €4,300, an effective rate of just over 0.2%.

(**Remember:** householders for properties in this bracket, once they go over the €1 million valuation mark, cannot rely on Revenue guidelines to value their properties without challenge.)

Section 17 also provides for a special treatment for properties owned by Local Authorities. For the valuation date 2013, all local authority properties will be deemed to be valued between €0–€100,000 and thereby in the lowest LPT bracket. This, however, is a temporary relief in that, as we have seen, the valuation date 2013 will cease to be relevant in 2017.

Section 18 – No Aggregation of Chargeable Values

Section 18 provides that each property owned by a liable person is to be considered separately. The property values are not aggregated for the purposes of arriving at the amount the liable person has to pay. This is important, because once a property value goes over €1 million, the tax rate increases. Three properties valued at €500,000 each are each charged individually to tax using the valuation band system.

Section 19 – Local Adjustment Factor
Section 20 – Power of Elected Members of Local Authority to Vary Basic Rates
Section 21 – Notification of Local Adjustment Factor to the Revenue Commissioners

Sections 19, 20 and 21 give local authorities the power to vary the rate of LPT. Section 19 defines both the 0.18% rate and the 0.25% rate as the "basic rate". Section 20 empowers the local authority to change this "basic rate" by the "local adjustment factor".

A local authority must go through a series of procedures before it can vary the basic rate. The local authority must follow any regulations laid down by the Minister for the Environment, Community and Local Government and these regulations might include requirements such as public consultation processes. Furthermore, the basic rate can only be adjusted by a local adjustment factor of 15% in either direction, which means that the maximum adjustment to the 0.18% rate that can be imposed by a local authority is to bring it up to 0.207%, and the minimum it can be reduced to is 0.153%. Similarly, the 0.25% rate can be adjusted to a maximum of 0.2875% and to a minimum of 0.2125%. The local authority is required to notify Revenue about the new rate it is imposing.

Part 5 – Care and Management

Section 22 – Care and Management of Local Property Tax

This section places LPT under the "care and management" of the Revenue Commissioners. It also applies Part 37 of TCA 1997 to LPT. Part 37 contains the administrative provisions of the TCA 1997, which provide a framework for the collection of taxes.

Section 23 – Delegation of Acts and Functions of Revenue Commissioners

This is purely an administrative section, allowing the Revenue Commissioners to delegate powers to their own officers.

Section 24 – "Electronic Means"

This allows for electronic filing and electronic transmission of information.

Section 25 – Combined Forms

This section allows Revenue to use combined forms, for example, a single return to be used for income tax and for LPT, should the need arise. Its purpose is to allow close integration between the LPT system and the general tax collection system.

Section 26 – Repayment of Local Property Tax

Section 26 allows for a repayment to be made in the case of an over-payment by reason of an error or a mistake in the LPT return. Any repayment is contingent on:

- the making of a claim for repayment within four years after the end of the year in which the liability date fell, *and*
- a complete return has been made, along with any other information which the Revenue might require to compute the repayment due.

Repayments can be made directly to the financial institution specified by the taxpayer. If a taxpayer is not happy with the repayment decision, he can take the matter to appeal.

Part 6 – The Register

Section 27 – The Register

This section provides that Revenue shall establish and maintain a register of residential properties, along with an associated list of the liable person in respect of each property. Revenue has a duty to maintain the register as accurately as possible.

Section 28 – Obligation to Register

Section 29 – Registration by Delivery of Return

These sections oblige liable persons to register with the Revenue Commissioners for LPT purposes and section 29 provides that registration is done through making a return.

Section 30 – Notification of Changes

This section requires taxpayers to notify the Revenue Commissioners of any relevant changes to be applied to the register, e.g. change of liable person or residential property.

Section 31 – Joint Owners of Property

This clarifies that the requirement to notify the Revenue Commissioners of any changes lies with the designated liable person in the case of a joint ownership.

Section 32– Evidence in Legal Proceedings

Section 32 is an administrative requirement, providing that a certificate signed by Revenue as to the contents of the register shall be accepted as proof in a court, unless the contrary can be proven. In essence, the burden of proof in establishing that there was a mistake in the register lies with the taxpayer, and not Revenue.

Part 7 – Returns

Section 33 – Issue of Notice by Revenue Requiring Returns to be Made

Section 33 allows Revenue to ask for a return, either from the liable person as per the register, or where they have reason to believe that a person should be a liable person. No liable person has to deliver a return earlier than the return date.

Section 34 – Claim that Person not a Liable Person

This deals with situations where a request for a return is incorrectly sent to someone who is not a liable person. In such situations, the person is obliged to notify Revenue, in writing, within 30 days of the date of the notification that they are not the liable person. They will have to explain why they are not the liable person and show documentary evidence, if available, to that effect. Additionally, they must also provide other information they might have as to who *is* the liable person. A right of appeal is available where Revenue does not agree.

Section 35 – Obligation on Liable Person to Prepare and Deliver a Return

Section 35 is key to the self-assessment nature of LPT. It provides that every liable person has to provide a return, even if not requested to do so.

Subsection (2) of this section goes on to provide that the liable person will not have to make a return in respect of the liability dates 1 November in 2013, 2014 and 2015, as long as a return was made for the liability date 1 May 2013 and the tax is paid in respect of each year. This is an important relieving provision from the obligation to make a return every year. Essentially, it provides that the return made in 2013 is valid for the next four years including 2013. It ties back to the provision in section 13 which allows the valuation used in respect of the valuation date on 1 May 2013 to persist for the first four years of operation of the LPT, i.e. for 2013, 2014, 2015 and 2016, the valuation date will always be 1 May 2013. Thus, once a return is made in 2013, the next due date for a return in the normal course of events will be 2017, made by reference to the liability date 1 November 2016. However, if a claim is made for deferral, a return must be made every year.

A change of ownership does not of itself automatically trigger the necessity to make a return within the three-year period. However, where a person who acquires a property has been given details of the valuation used by the previous owner who was the liable person, and it appears that the valuation previously used was unreasonable, the new liable person must make a return.

Also, specific provision is made to ensure that if a property is acquired from a buyer who purchased the property in year 2013 (and therefore that property would have been exempt) the person acquiring the property becomes the liable person for the property and must make a return.

Underlying this section giving relief from the making of an annual return is the underlying presumption that any payment arrangements specified in the original return will continue to apply across the three-year period.

Section 36 – Preparation and Delivery of Return by Person Acting under Authority

Many people who will be liable to LPT will not be used to making tax returns. Section 36 allows a liable person to have returns made, on their behalf and under their authority, by somebody else.

Section 37 – Company Returns

If the liable person is a company, the LPT return has to be prepared and delivered by the company secretary.

Section 38 – Surcharge for Late Submission of Income Tax and Corporation Tax Returns

Section 38 only applies to a person who is a "chargeable person" – normally someone who is self-employed or a company. The section links the filing requirements for the Form 11 income tax return with the LPT return. If you have not filed the LPT return for the year (if one was required) or if you have not paid the LPT before you file Form 11, the Form 11 return would be deemed to be two months late. Where the Form 11 is two months late, the penalty surcharge of 10% of the income tax payable is applied to your income tax liability, subject to a maximum increased amount of €63,485. This is a very serious penalty, and can only be mitigated by filing any outstanding LPT returns and paying any outstanding LPT. Where that is done, the penalty surcharge is limited to the amount of LPT at issue. The section also provides that if the Form 11 income tax return was late in any event, and the surcharge was applied, the surcharge will not be increased by reason of the LPT return being late.

Section 39 – Particulars to be Included in a Return

This sets out the items that may be requested by the Revenue Commissioners in an LPT return. They include the obvious things like the address of the property and the chargeable value, but also the PPSN or tax reference number of the taxpayer. This underlines the close links between LPT and the mainstream income tax system.

Section 40 – Self-assessment and Signed Declaration

The LPT return is a self-assessment return and must contain a signed declaration by the preparer that the return is, to the best of the person's knowledge and belief, correct. *Note*: in completing the return, it is the preparer (and not necessarily the liable person) who must certify that the return is, to the best of their knowledge, correct.

Section 41 – Method of Payment and Deferral

It is the person who prepares the return who selects the payment method, and also who elects to defer the payment if the liable person is eligible for deferral.

Where an election to pay LPT by one of the methods specified in the return is made, but without including a self-assessment of the amount to be paid, the method selected will be applied to paying the Revenue estimate.

Section 42 – One Return in Respect of Jointly Owned Property

Only one return is to be made per property. Where there is more than one liable person, the contents of the return will bind all the liable persons. Where Revenue has received more than one return on a property, they will accept the return made by the designated liable person and notify this to the other person making the return. If more than one return is received in respect of a property for which there is no one designated liable person, it is up to Revenue to decide who the designated liable person is.

Section 43 – Designated Liable Person

This section builds on section 42. Its purpose is to determine who the designated liable person is when there is more than one liable person. Revenue can specify who the designated liable person should be, but outside of that, the designated liable person is the first person to meet the first applicable condition in the following list:

1. the person elected by the other liable persons to be the designated liable person;
2. the person who paid the household charge on the property (if it arose);
3. the person who paid the non-principal private residence (NPPR) charge on the property (if it arose);
4. for a married couple or civil partnership who are jointly assessed, the assessable person for income tax purposes;
5. where the property is owned by a partnership, the Precedent Acting partner;
6. the person with the highest total income for tax purposes;
7. where a company and an individual own the property between them, the individual is the designated liable person;
8. where some of the owners are not resident for tax purposes, the owner that is resident is the designated liable person.

Section 44 – Electronic Delivery of Returns

We have seen above (*section 24*) that the legislation permits the submission of returns by electronic means. Under section 44, some taxpayers are *obliged* to submit their returns electronically. These are:

- persons who are liable for more than one residential property; and
- persons who are already obliged to file their income tax or corporation tax returns electronically.

Section 45 – Evidence of Failure to Deliver a Return

An administrative section providing that a certificate signed by Revenue (after examining their relevant records) identifying a liable person who has not filed an LPT return, shall be proof of non-filing until, and if, the contrary is proved otherwise.

Section 46 – Return by Agents and Lessees

This section involves Revenue's power of inquiry (see **Section 7.4.2**). Revenue can oblige letting agents to provide details of the owners of residential properties which are managed by them as letting agents. Conversely, Revenue can oblige a lessee or occupier to provide details of the terms of their lease or letting agreement, and details in relation to the lessor of the property. While a penalty of €1,000 shall apply for failure to comply with a Revenue request of this nature, it is provided that any failure to comply will not be treated as a criminal offence. Most breaches of the tax code can be escalated as criminal offences if the failure to comply is sufficiently severe, but not this one. Furthermore, Revenue must have reasonable grounds for the inquiry in the first instance.

Part 8 – Revenue Estimates and Assessments

Section 47 – Making of Revenue Estimates

Revenue may make estimates of LPT due as regards a relevant residential property and must notify the taxpayer if they do so.

Section 48 – Amendment of Revenue Estimate

Revenue may amend their estimates up or down, and must notify the taxpayer.

Section 49 – Revenue Estimate becomes Due and Payable

If the taxpayer is notified of a Revenue estimate, and a return containing a self-assessment and an election for specified method of payment is not delivered, the Revenue estimate becomes due and payable.

Section 50 – Displacement of Revenue Estimate by Self-assessment

Where an LPT return is made and a payment option provided, the Revenue estimate will cease to apply. If any LPT has already been paid on foot of the Revenue estimate, it would be offset against the self-assessment. Any amount to be repaid will be repaid, but subject to Revenue being satisfied that the taxpayer does not owe tax under any other head of charge. If taxes are owed, the LPT refund will first go against any other taxes owing.

Section 51 – Claim by Person Notified of Estimate that He or She is not a Liable Person

Revenue's estimate will also be discharged if the taxpayer has established that they are not the liable person in relation to the estimate.

Section 52 – Self-assessment

This section defines self-assessment for LPT. It is the assessment by a liable person in a return, or by a person acting under the authority of the liable person, of the amount of LPT payable.

Section 53 – Local Property Tax Payable in Accordance with Self-assessment

Section 53 states that the LPT liability is the amount of the self-assessment.

Section 54 – Revenue Assessment

Earlier sections of the Act have dealt with the making of estimates by Revenue, which could be displaced by the taxpayer's self-assessment. Section 54 sets out the circumstances of Revenue making its own assessments. Revenue can raise an assessment on either a liable person or a person whom Revenue believe is the liable person. While the assessment has to take account of LPT already paid, the assessment may relate to more than one property for which the taxpayer is liable.

Section 55 – Making of Revenue Assessment

Revenue can raise an assessment where neither an estimate nor a taxpayer self-assessment has been made, or where the Revenue believes that the taxpayer's self-assessment was insufficient.

Section 56 – Notice of Assessment

This deals with the form of the assessment, and is largely administrative. The assessment has to be notified to the taxpayer along with a note of the time allowed for making an appeal. The assessment may also include the chargeable value of the property, the LPT payable and the name and address of the Revenue officer dealing with the case.

Section 57 – Amendment of a Revenue Assessment

Revenue can amend assessments at any time, always providing that they let the taxpayer know.

Section 58 – Time Limits for Making Assessments

Revenue cannot make an assessment before the return date. Where a properly completed return has been made, no Revenue assessment shall be made, no additional LPT will be due and no LPT will be repaid after the end of four years commencing on 1 January following the year in which the relevant liability date falls. Where a taxpayer believes that Revenue are out of time on making an assessment, this can only be substantiated by way of appeal to the Appeal Commissioners.

However, Revenue can change an assessment at any stage even outside the four years where they find that the return was not correct, or where the outcome of an appeal must be given effect, or simply to correct the calculation. Where this situation arises additional LPT can be levied, but likewise LPT overpaid can be repaid.

Section 59 – Appeals against Revenue Assessments

Section 59 sets out the rules for appealing against assessments. The general rule is that a taxpayer can appeal a Revenue assessment by giving notice in writing to Revenue within 30 days of the date of the assessment that they wish to appeal.

An appeal cannot be made, however, until the LPT return for the period has been submitted and the amount of LPT due in the self-assessment paid. Revenue is obliged to refuse an application for an appeal unless these conditions are met within 30 days of the date of the assessment being appealed. The Appeal Commissioners will, in the first instance, determine whether or not the Revenue officer was entitled to make the assessment. If Revenue were not prohibited from raising the assessment, then the assessment can be appealed again on other grounds.

Section 60 – Claim that Person not a Liable Person

Taxpayers who receive a notice of assessment and who do not believe they are the liable person can appeal as if they were the liable person.

Part 9 – Appeals

Section 61 – Appeals against Revenue Assessments

The determination of the appeal by the Appeal Commissioners shall be final and conclusive, unless the matter is taken either to the Circuit Court or to the High Court on a point of law.

Section 62 – Application and Modification of Part 40 of the Act of 1997

This section ensures that the general rules applicable to appeal hearings for income tax also apply to LPT. One particular point to emphasise is that the outcome of appeal hearings may be published. Under the rules for publication of appeal hearings by the Appeal Commissioners, details have to be removed so that taxpayers concerned cannot be identified.

Section 63 – Power to Issue Precepts

This is a purely technical section, which allows for certain information in connection with an appeal to be provided to the Appeal Commissioners.

Part 10 – Deduction at Source

Chapter 1 – Deduction by Employers and Pension Providers

It is necessary to establish special rules to enable Revenue to operate the deduction of LPT at source. The first set of rules involves the most commonly occurring instance of tax deduction at source, namely the PAYE system.

Section 64 – Interpretation (Chapter 1)

This is a definitions section. The most important definition is that concerning "net emoluments". *Net emoluments* means take-home pay – what is left from gross pay after the deduction of PAYE income tax, PRSI and the Universal Social Charge. There could also be a pre-existing Court Order requiring a deduction from wages, perhaps in the context of a separation arrangement, which would serve to reduce net emoluments further.

Section 65 – Direction to Employer to Deduct Local Property Tax

Revenue may instruct an employer to withhold LPT from net emoluments – that is to say, LPT is paid from after-tax income. Where a person changes his or her job, Revenue can direct the new employer to deduct any balance of LPT still outstanding. *Note*: taxpayer confidentiality does not apply to any direction made by Revenue to any employer under this section.

Section 66 – Circumstances in which Local Property Tax to be Deducted

This section sets out the four circumstances in which the deduction of LPT at source through payroll will be applied. The first is obvious: when the taxpayer *elects* on their LPT return to have the LPT deducted. Revenue, however, can decide to have the LPT deducted from payroll if the taxpayer's return did not specify any method of payment, or if the taxpayer has defaulted in making payment by another method. Lastly, the taxpayer can agree with Revenue to have any LPT arising as a consequence of a Revenue assessment withheld from his or her salary. An assessment may arise where no LPT return was filed and Revenue "assesses" the taxpayer for the tax due.

Section 67 – Notification to Liable Person that Direction Given to Employer

Where Revenue use the two powers of collection enforcement through payroll available to them under section 66, i.e. where the taxpayer's return did not specify any method of payment or where the taxpayer defaulted in making payment by another method, they are obliged to notify the taxpayer that they are doing so.

Section 68 – Deduction by Employer in Subsequent Periods

This section envisages that the taxpayer will want to leave the payroll withholding arrangement in place from year to year.

Section 69 – Amount of Local Property Tax to be Deducted

In this section it is specified how much Revenue can oblige an employer to deduct from a taxpayer's salary. Essentially, it is the amount of the self-assessment or the amount of the Revenue assessment, as the case may be, and can include any LPT unpaid from previous years and any interest due on late payments, but must take account of any payments already made.

Section 70 – Revised Direction to Employer

Revenue can give a revised instruction to an employer to deduct the LPT in several circumstances. These are where:

- the employee settles some or all of the LPT directly; or
- the employee ceases to be employed by the employer deducting the LPT; or
- a deferral is claimed (see **Chapter 5**); or
- the LPT amount set out in the direction for collection is incorrect; or
- a recent self-assessment does not concur with amounts currently being withheld.

Section 71 – Withdrawal of Direction on Request from Liable Person

The taxpayer can ask Revenue at any time that LPT payments not be withheld from his or her salary or wages. Revenue, however, has the right to refuse this request if the taxpayer does not agree an alternative payment method, or where a true and complete return is outstanding, or, more generally, where Revenue consider that suspending the collection of LPT at source would affect timely collection of LPT.

Section 72 – Deduction by Employer

A taxpayer's employer can only deduct LPT with the same frequency as the taxpayer receives a salary or wages, nor can the employer deduct LPT if there are insufficient wages to cover the liability.

Withholding is to be done in instalments (see **Section 4.4.1**). The LPT payments are to be spread evenly across whatever number of paydays arise between the employer receiving the notification of withholding and the end of the period for which the Revenue directions are given.

Section 72 recognises that wage and salary payments can vary from payday to payday, and that it is possible that for some paydays there would be an insufficient amount of wages from which to deduct the LPT due on the particular date. Where this happens, Revenue must be notified by the employer and the shortfall has to be made up across any remaining paydays in the period.

Section 73 – Cessation of Employment

If a taxpayer, who pays LPT in instalments under the payroll system, leaves their employment, the employer must immediately send Revenue a statement of the payments already withheld. This is part of the P45 procedure.

Section 74 – Payment of Local Property Tax Deducted by Employer

Employers are required to send to the Collector General the amounts of LPT withheld, just as if it were PAYE.

Section 75 – Failure by Employer to Remit Local Property Tax

Revenue can issue an employer with a notification or a demand if the employer does not pay the amount of LPT withheld from any employees.

Section 76 – Under-deduction of Local Property Tax by Employer

This section provides that even if the employer were not correctly deducting LPT from payroll, the employee is still liable for LPT. Revenue is empowered to agree an alternative payment method for LPT directly with the taxpayer.

Section 77 – Over-deduction of Local Property Tax by Employer

This is a simple administration section. It enables Revenue to repay any over-deducted LPT to the liable person.

Section 78 – Deduction from Net Emoluments of Certain Company Directors

The tax code already contains a special measure to ensure that the PAYE operated on a company director who has a "material interest" in the company, will not be credited against such directors' personal tax liability, unless it can be shown that not only did the company deduct the PAYE, it also paid it over to the Collector General. Broadly, a *material interest* involves being able to own or control more than 15% of the ordinary share capital of a company. Section 78 transposes this measure to LPT, where an LPT payment deducted from salary will not be credited against the liability of a director with a material interest unless it can be shown that the LPT withheld from payroll was actually paid over to the Collector General.

Section 79 – Return by Employer at End of Year

This section makes arrangements for annual returns to be made by employers to the Collector General on LPT withheld, in a fashion similar to the P35 system for PAYE.

Section 80 – End of Year Statement of Deductions to be Given to a Liable Person

This makes arrangements for annual statements to be given by employers to employees on LPT withheld, similar to the P60 system for PAYE.

Section 81 – Employer to Keep Records

This obliges employers to retain records of LPT withheld for a period of six years.

Section 82 – Employer Treated as if Net Emoluments Paid to a Liable Person

Section 82 ensures that an employer is indemnified against any charge of underpaying employees merely because of the correct deduction of LPT.

Chapter 2 – Deduction by Minister for Social Protection

Section 83 – Interpretation (Chapter 2)

This is a definitions section. The social welfare schemes from which LPT may be deducted are defined by reference to sections 39 and 139 of the Social Welfare Consolidation Act 2005. The "net scheme payments" are those DSP amounts payable after any deductions under section 341(7) of the 2005 Act or under a Court Order requiring a deduction from the social welfare payments.

Section 84 – Direction to Minister to Deduct Local Property Tax

Revenue may direct the Minister to deduct LPT from any net scheme payments payable to a liable person. Where a taxpayer is benefiting from more than one Department of Social Protection scheme, Revenue must direct the withholding of LPT from just one scheme.

Section 85 – Circumstances in which Direction to Deduct Local Property Tax may be Given

As per section 66, this section sets out the four circumstances in which the deduction of LPT at source through net scheme payments will be applied:

1. The liable person elects, on their LPT return, to have LPT deducted.
2. Revenue decides to have LPT deducted if the liable person's return did not specify any method of payment.
3. The liable person defaulted in making payment by another method.
4. The liable person can agree with Revenue to have any LPT arising as a consequence of a Revenue assessment withheld.

Otherwise the arrangements made for deduction of LPT from social welfare payments are virtually identical to the arrangements made for deduction of LPT from salaries and wages. There are some important differences, however (see *section 92*).

Section 86 – Election for Specific Method of Payment

Where a liable person elects to have LPT deducted from a particular DSP scheme, Revenue will collect the amounts due from that scheme except where to do so would adversely affect the timely collection of the LPT. If that is deemed to be the case, Revenue can direct that the LPT is collected from some other scheme or Revenue may select a different payment method other than from net scheme payments.

Section 87 – Notification to Liable Person that Direction given to Minister

Where Revenue use the two powers of collection enforcement through net scheme payments available to them under section 85, i.e. where the liable person's return did not specify any method of payment, or where the liable person defaulted in making payment by another method, Revenue is obliged to notify the liable person that they are doing so.

Section 88 – Deduction by Minister in Subsequent Periods

Where a liable person does not withdraw his or her consent to have LPT deducted from net scheme payments, deduction of LPT from net scheme payments will continue for subsequent periods.

Section 89 – Withdrawal of Direction on Request from Liable Person

The liable person can ask Revenue at any time that LPT payments not be withheld from net scheme payments. Revenue, however, has the right to refuse this request if the liable person does not agree an alternative payment method, or where a true and complete return is outstanding, or more generally where Revenue consider that suspending the collection of LPT at source would affect the timely collection of LPT.

Section 90 – Amount of Local Property Tax to be Deducted

In this section it is specified how much LPT Revenue can oblige the Minister to deduct. Essentially, it is the amount of the self-assessment or the amount of the Revenue assessment, as the case may be, and can include any LPT unpaid from previous years and any interest due on late payments, but must take account of any payments already made.

Section 91 – Revised Direction to Minister

Revenue can give a revised instruction to the Minister to deduct LPT in several circumstances. These are where:

- the liable person settles some or all of the LPT due directly; or
- the liable person ceases to receive net scheme payments from the Minister deducting LPT; or
- a deferral is claimed; or
- the LPT amount set out in the direction for collection is incorrect; or

- a recent self-assessment does not concur with amounts currently being withheld.

Section 92 – Deduction by Minister

The amount of LPT withheld from a scheme cannot be such as to reduce the payment below the weekly rate of Supplementary Welfare Allowance of €186. It is the liable person's responsibility to ensure that the amount deducted each week from the social welfare payment will meet his LPT liability. If the Minister is unable to deduct LPT from the net scheme payments whereby the deduction would bring the net scheme payment below €186 per week, the Minister for Social Protection is required to notify Revenue.

Section 93 – Remittance of Local Property Tax Deducted by the Minister to the Revenue Commissioners

Generally speaking, the Department of Social Protection will have to remit any LPT withheld from a payment within seven days of the making of the payment.

Section 94 – Information to be Provided to the Revenue Commissioners

The Minister shall send to the Revenue Commissioners details of LPT deductions made in the manner agreed.

Section 95 – Cessation of Scheme Payments

Where a person ceases to be a beneficiary of the social welfare scheme from which the LPT payments are being withheld, the Minister for Social Protection is required to notify Revenue.

Section 96 – Under-deduction of Local Property Tax by Minister

This section provides that if the Minister does not correctly deduct LPT from net scheme payments, Revenue is empowered to agree an alternative payment method for LPT directly with the liable person; or Revenue may direct the Minister to deduct any unpaid amounts from subsequent payments.

Section 97 – Over-deduction of Local Property Tax by Minister

In the event of an over-deduction of LPT by the Minister, it is Revenue and not the Minister who shall repay the excess amount to the liable person.

Section 98 – Statement of Deductions

A liable person may request a statement of total LPT deductions from the Minister at the period end.

Section 99 – Minister to Keep Records

The Minister must keep records of:

- the net scheme payments of the liable person;
- the LPT deducted from such payments;
- the details of remittance of such deductions to the Revenue Commissioners.

The Minister is obliged to keep these records for a period of six years from the end of the year to which they relate.

Section 100 – Minister Treated as if Net Scheme Payments paid to a Liable Person

Section 100 ensures that the Minister is indemnified against any charge of underpaying net scheme payments to a liable person merely because of the correct deduction of LPT.

It can be seen from these arrangements that, in practice, there will be very tight integration between the State's operation of social welfare benefits and its tax collection mechanisms.

Chapter 3 – Deduction by Minister for Agriculture, Food and the Marine

This chapter of the Act involves a further transposition of the collection at source rules, this time to payments made by the Department of Agriculture, Food and the Marine.

Section 101 – Interpretation (Chapter 3)

This is a definitions section. The schemes from which LPT may be deducted are defined by reference to schemes specified in the

Schedule to the Agricultural Appeals Act 2001. The *net scheme payments* are those amounts payable after any debt due to the Minister or under a Court Order requiring a deduction from net scheme payments.

Section 102 – Direction to Minister to Deduct Local Property Tax

Revenue may direct the Minister to deduct LPT from any net scheme payments payable to a liable person.

Section 103 – Circumstances in which Direction to Deduct Local Property Tax may be Given

As per section 66 (see above), section 103 sets out the four circumstances in which the deduction of LPT at source through net scheme payments will be applied:

1. The liable person elects, on their LPT return, to have LPT deducted from the net scheme payments.
2. Revenue decides to have LPT deducted if the liable person's return did not specify any method of payment.
3. The liable person defaulted in making payment by another method.
4. The liable person can agree with Revenue to have any LPT arising as a consequence of a Revenue assessment withheld.

Section 104 – Election for Specific Method of Payment

Where a liable person elects to have LPT deducted from net scheme payments, Revenue will collect the amounts due from that scheme except where to do so would adversely affect the timely collection of the LPT. If that is deemed to be the case, Revenue may select a different payment method other than from net scheme payments.

Section 105 – Notification to Liable Person that Direction given to the Minister

Where Revenue use the two powers of collection enforcement through net scheme payments available to them under section 103, that is, where the liable person's return did not specify any method of payment, or where the liable person defaulted in making payment by another method, Revenue is obliged to notify the liable person that they are doing so.

Section 106 – Deduction by the Minister in Subsequent Periods

Where a liable person does not withdraw his or her consent to have LPT deducted from net scheme payments, deduction of LPT from net scheme payments will continue for subsequent periods.

Section 107 – Withdrawal of Direction on Request from Liable Person

The liable person can request Revenue at any time that LPT payments not be withheld from net scheme payments. Revenue, however, has the right to refuse this request if the liable person does not agree an alternative payment method or where a true and complete return is outstanding, or, more generally, where Revenue consider that suspending the collection of LPT at source would affect the timely collection of LPT.

Section 108 – Amount of Local Property Tax to be Deducted

Here it is specified how much Revenue can oblige the Minister to deduct. Essentially, it is the amount of the self-assessment or the amount of the Revenue assessment as the case may be, and can include any LPT unpaid from previous years and any interest due on late payments, but must take account of any payments already made.

Section 109 – Revised Direction to Minister

Revenue can give a revised instruction to the Minister to deduct LPT in several circumstances. These are where:

- the liable person settles some or all of LPT due directly; or
- the liable person ceases to receive net scheme payments from the Minister deducting LPT; or
- a deferral is claimed; or
- the LPT amount set out in the direction for collection is incorrect; or
- a recent self-assessment does not concur with amounts currently being withheld.

Section 110 – Deduction by Minister

Where the Minister is unable to deduct the full amount of LPT due from the net scheme payments due to insufficient net scheme payments, the Minister must collect any amount of LPT that can be covered by the scheme payments. There is no minimum floor, as is the case with social welfare net scheme payments.

Section 111 – Remittance of Local Property Tax Deducted by the Minister to the Revenue Commissioners

Generally speaking, the Department of Agriculture, Marine and Food will have to remit any LPT withheld from a payment within seven days of the making of the payment.

Section 112 – Information to be Provided to the Revenue Commissioners

The Minister shall send to the Revenue Commissioners details of LPT deductions made in the manner agreed.

Section 113 – Under-deduction of Local Property Tax by Minister

This section provides that if the Minister does not correctly deduct LPT from net scheme payments, Revenue is empowered to agree an alternative payment method for LPT directly with the liable person; or Revenue may direct the Minister to deduct any unpaid amounts from subsequent payments.

Section 114 – Over-deduction of Local Property Tax by Minister

In the event of an over-deduction of LPT by the Minister, it is Revenue and not the Minister who shall repay the excess amount to the liable person.

Section 115 – Statement of Deductions

A liable person may request a statement of total LPT deductions from the Minister at the period end.

Section 116 – Minister to Keep Records

The Minister must keep records of:

- the net scheme payments of the liable person;
- the LPT deducted from such payments;
- the details of remittance of such deductions to Revenue.

The Minister is obliged to keep these records for a period of six years from the end of the year to which they relate.

Section 117 – Minister Treated as if Net Scheme Payments Paid to a Liable Person

This section ensures that the Minister is indemnified against any charge of underpaying net scheme payments to a liable person merely because of the correct deduction of LPT.

Chapter 4 – Deduction from State Payments

Section 118 – Deduction of Local Property Tax from State Payments

Section 118 provides that LPT may be deducted from any state payment, subject to agreed arrangements between the Minister for Finance and any other government minister being put in place. At the time of writing, no such additional arrangements are in force.

Part 11 – Collection and Enforcement

Section 119 – Date for Payment of Local Property Tax

This section specifies the dates for the payment of LPT. These are:

- 1 July 2013, in respect of the liability date 1 May 2013; and
- 1 January, in respect of the liability date 1 November in any other year.

As 1 January is a public holiday, for practical purposes, the payment date would be the first working day thereafter. Payments deducted through payroll shall be paid over to the Collector General in accordance with the time limits imposed under PAYE/PRSI rules (i.e. payable by the 23rd of the month after the payment month) and within seven days from the payment of the net scheme amount where LPT is paid by deduction from payments from the Department of Social Protection (DSP) or the Department of Agriculture, Food and the Marine (DAFM).

Section 120 – Collection and Recovery of Local Property Tax

This section provides that Revenue has the same powers of collection and collection enforcement it has for all other taxes.

Section 121 – Revenue Commissioners may Decide on Allocation of Payment

Where LPT is payable by a taxpayer on more than one property, Revenue can decide the allocation of the LPT payments across the properties. This might occur, for example, in the case of a shortfall or in the case of outstanding amounts for back years.

Section 122 – Third Party Payment Service Providers

This is a technical section to deal with payments made by taxpayers via third parties, e.g. credit card companies. It permits Revenue to accept payment less the commission charged by the company, but it also makes the service provider liable for amounts paid to it by a liable person in settlement or part-settlement of an LPT liability.

Section 123 – Unpaid Amount to be a Charge on Property

If any LPT, interest or penalty remains unpaid, it will remain a charge on the property to which it relates. The practical implication of this is that on a sale of the property title cannot pass until any outstanding amounts are settled with Revenue.

Section 124 – No Time Limit on Charge

This ensures that the Statute of Limitations will not apply to charges on property derived from unpaid LPT or interest or penalties.

Section 125 – Meaning of "Sale"

This section clarifies that for LPT purposes, the sale of property includes a sale under a compulsory purchase order, or a sale at undervalue, or a gift.

Section 126 – Liable Person to Pay Unpaid Local Property Tax on Sale of Property

Any liable person who proposes to sell a property is obliged to pay to Revenue, before the completion of the sale, any LPT owed, deferred or penalties or interest which may have accrued on the property.

Section 127 – Unpaid Local Property Tax to Remain as a Charge on Property

Where the liable person does not pay the LPT amounts owed to Revenue before completion of a sale, any unpaid amounts remain as a charge on the property even in the case of a new owner. The charge is on the property rather than on the individual.

Section 127A – Charges on Property Following Sale

Where a residential property is sold and the new liable person makes an LPT return in respect of the first liability date after the sale, LPT outstanding at the date of sale ceases to be a charge on the said residential property.

Section 128 – Confirmation that Local Property Tax Paid

Revenue will provide a liable person, or someone acting on his or her behalf, with confirmation of all amounts due on a property at the time of a sale of the property or confirmation that no amounts are due.

Section 129 – Tax Clearance Certificates and Deferred Local Property Tax

A person shall be deemed to be tax compliant and entitled to a tax clearance certificate under section 1095 of TCA 1997 where the only amount of tax outstanding is LPT that has been deferred in accordance with the Act (see **Chapter 5**).

Part 12 – Deferred Payment of Local Property Tax

Section 130 – Interpretation (Part 12)

This is the definitions section and includes definitions that may not be in common usage within the meaning of LPT heretofore. For example, "relevant event" in relation to LPT means the sale of a property by a liable person who has claimed a deferral or the completion of an insolvency arrangement; and "windfall" which is defined as winnings, gifts, inheritances and capital sums of any kind. *Note*: there is no monetary value specified.

Section 131 – Meaning of Deferral

A claim for deferral will be valid if the conditions for deferral are met and the claim was made in writing and an LPT return is filed in respect of each liability date. Where a valid claim for deferral is made, LPT will not be payable until the property is sold and the amount deferred will include any accrued interest payable at a daily rate of 0.011% (4% p.a.).

Section 132 – Income Threshold for Deferral

This section sets out the income thresholds that determine whether a deferral can be claimed on income grounds. These are:
For a full deferral:

- not exceeding €15,000 per annum for a single person;
- not exceeding €25,000 per annum for a married couple, civil partners or cohabitants.

For a partial 50% deferral:

- not exceeding €25,000 per annum for a single person;
- not exceeding €35,000 per annum for a married couple, civil partners or cohabitants.

Section 133 – Income Threshold Increased by Mortgage Payment

The threshold amounts are increased by an amount of 80% of the gross mortgage interest amount payable on the liable person's main or sole residence.

Section 133A – Personal Representatives

The personal representatives of a deceased liable person may claim a deferral of any LPT and interest already deferred by the deceased liable person until such time as the property is sold and the proceeds distributed or the property is transferred to a beneficiary or after three years from the date of death.

Section 133B – Personal Insolvency Act 2012

Where a liable person enters into an insolvency arrangement under the Personal Insolvency Act 2012, the liable person may qualify for a deferral of LPT for the period of the insolvency arrangement.

Section 133C – Excessive Financial Hardship

Where a liable person suffers an unexpected, significant financial loss or expense and where payment of LPT may cause significant hardship, Revenue may consider a claim, in writing, for a deferral.

Section 134 – Continuation of Deferral

If the liable person ceases to meet the criteria for income threshold, personal insolvency, personal representatives or excessive financial loss, any deferral allowed before the criteria ceased shall continue, provided that the liable person was entitled to the deferral in the first instance. Where a spouse, civil partner or cohabitant dies, the liable person may continue to claim the deferral until the next valuation date, notwithstanding that the surviving person no longer satisfies the deferral thresholds.

Section 135 – Appeal against Revenue Determination that Liable Person not Entitled to Deferral

Where Revenue determine that a liable person is not eligible for a deferral, they must inform that person in writing and the liable person may appeal that determination by giving notice, in writing, within 14 days of the determination being made.

Section 136 – *Payments made against Deferred Amount*

A liable person who has been allowed a deferral can make a full or partial payment against the deferred amount at any time. Revenue is obliged to credit such payments against the earliest amounts due.

Section 137 – *Charge on Property*

The deferred amount shall be and continue to be a charge on the property to which it relates until the property is sold. There is no time limit on the continuation of the charge.

Section 138 – *Limit on Deferred Amount*

LPT deferred cannot exceed the chargeable value of the property at the liability date.

Section 139 – *Occurrence of Relevant Events*

Any deferred amount becomes payable where the property is sold or transferred or where the liable person is in receipt of a windfall gain. However, in the case of a transfer of the property by way of gift or inheritance, Revenue may allow the deferral to continue if the new liable person makes a valid claim for a deferral.

Part 13 – Revenue Powers

Section 140 [section deleted]

Section 141 – *Right of Revenue Officer to make Inquiries*

This section allows a Revenue officer to make inquiries as to whether:

- a property was a relevant residential property at the liability date and what its chargeable value was on a valuation date, or
- a person is a liable person and whether they are eligible for a deferral, or
- any return made is true and accurate,

within four years after any liability date.

Section 142 – Appeal against a Revenue Officer's Inquiries

A liable person can appeal any inquiry made by Revenue by giving notice, in writing, within 30 days of receipt of the inquiry and stating the grounds of the appeal. The Appeal Commissioners shall hear and treat the appeal in the same manner as an appeal against a Revenue assessment.

Section 143 [Section Deleted]

Section 144 – Inspection of Records Relating to Deduction at Source

Revenue has the power to inspect the records of those charged with the deduction of LPT at source. This includes employers, the Department of Social Protection and the Department of Agriculture, Food and the Marine.

Part 14 – Offences and Penalties

Section 145 – Penalties in Respect of Non-compliance with Part 10

Where a person fails to make or remit a deduction at source, or to keep, retain or supply records in accordance with the instructions set out by Revenue, he or she shall be liable to a penalty of €3,000.

Where a person fails to send an end of year statement to Revenue within the period specified, that person shall be liable for a penalty of €500 for each month in which the statement remains outstanding, subject to a maximum penalty of €3,000.

If the person referred to is a company secretary, the company secretary shall be liable to a separate penalty of €2,000.

Section 146 – Penalty for Failure to Deliver a Return

The penalty for the non-filing of an LPT return is equal to the amount of the LPT due, subject to a maximum penalty of €3,000. Where a person who is selling a property fails to pass on the details of the current valuation for LPT purposes to the new liable person, the previous owner is liable to a penalty of €500.

Section 147 – Penalty for False Statement or False Representation

The penalty for making a false statement or for filing an incorrect LPT return is an amount equal to the LPT due subject to a maximum penalty of €3,000.

Section 147A – Assessment as Evidence of Amount of Tax Payable

Where an assessment cannot be varied by the courts or by the Appeal Commissioners, this assessment is evidence of the amount of LPT due.

Section 148 – Application of Certain Provisions of TCA 1997

This applies the provisions of Part 47 of TCA 1997 to the penalties envisaged by the LPTA 2013.

Section 149 – Interest on Overdue Tax

Interest on late payment of LPT is due at a rate of 0.0219% per day or part thereof.

Section 150 – Repayment of Interest

Where the payable amount of LPT is reduced after interest has been paid, the excess interest paid shall be refunded.

Part 15 – Information Required by the Revenue Commissioners

Section 151 – Information to be Provided to the Revenue Commissioners

Revenue may request a relevant person (see *section 153*) to furnish them with any information they may deem necessary for the administration of LPT and the maintenance of the property register.

Section 152 – Information to be Provided by the Revenue Commissioners

Revenue may provide any information (other than taxpayer information) to the Minister for Finance or the Minister for the Environment, Community and Local Government, which they may require.

Revenue may also provide information to a local authority to help identify and verify details of residential properties in the local authority area.

Section 153 – Relevant Persons

This section lists the relevant persons from whom Revenue may seek information for the establishment and maintenance of the property register and for the administration of LPT. These are:

(a) the Local Government Management Agency;
(b) the Property Registration Authority;
(c) the Private Residential Tenancies Board;
(d) electricity providers who hold a licence under the Electricity Regulation Act 1999;
(e) gas providers who hold a natural gas licence under the Gas (Interim) Regulation Act 2002;
(f) An Post;
(g) the Valuation Office;
(h) Ordnance Survey Ireland;
(i) the Minister for Social Protection;
(j) the Minister for Agriculture, Food and the Marine;
(k) the Minister for the Environment, Community and Local Government;
(l) the Minister for Communications, Energy and Natural Resources;
(m) the Minister for Transport, Tourism and Sport;
(n) any local authority;
(o) the Health Service Executive;
(p) the National Asset Management Agency; and
(q) the Sustainable Energy Authority of Ireland.

Part 16 – Household Charge

Section 154 – Interpretation (Part 16)

This section defines "liability to the household charge" as the liability amount of €100 plus any late payment and/or interest fee payable by a relevant person.

Section 155 – Cessation of Household Charge

The Household Charge ceases after 1 January 2013.

Section 156 – Arrears of Household Charge

Where amounts of Household Charge remain unpaid, the amount payable for arrears will rise to €130 if paid by 30 April 2013 to the local authority. Where Household Charge remains unpaid as of 1 July 2013, the liability to Household Charge is converted to an LPT charge of €200 and is payable to the Revenue Commissioners.

Part 17 – Supplementary Provisions

Section 157 – Transfer of Local Property Tax to the Local Government Fund

This provides for the transfer of LPT from Government central funds into the Local Government Fund giving legislative effect to the notion that LPT is a local tax to be used by the local authorities.

Section 158 – Amendment to the Act of 1997

Any provisions in the Finance (Local Property Tax) Act 2012, (as amended), amend the Taxes Consolidation Act 1997.

Section 159 – Extension of Certain Acts

This section ensures that the term "local property tax" is included in the Provisional Collection of Taxes Act 1927 and in the Inland Revenue Regulation Act 1890.

Index